For the Love of
Bob

Love Karen

About the Author

James Bowen is a street musician in London. He found Bob the cat in 2007 and the pair have been inseparable ever since.

For the Love
of Bob

James Bowen

HODDER

First published in Great Britain in 2014 by Hodder & Stoughton
An Hachette UK company

3

Copyright © James and Bob Ltd and Connected Content Ltd 2014

The right of James Bowen and Garry Jenkins to be identified as the
Authors of the Work has been asserted by them in accordance with the
Copyright, Designs and Patents Act 1988.

A CIP catalogue record for this title is available from the British Library

Paperback ISBN 978 1 444 79405 2
Ebook ISBN 978 1 444 79404 5

Typeset by Hewer Text UK Ltd, Edinburgh
Printed and bound by CPI Group (UK) Ltd, Croydon, CR0 4YY

Hodder & Stoughton policy is to use papers that are natural,
renewable and recyclable products and made from wood grown
in sustainable forests. The logging and manufacturing processes
are expected to conform to the environmental regulations
of the country of origin.

Hodder & Stoughton Ltd
338 Euston Road
London NW1 3BH

www.hodder.co.uk

To Garry, my mentor and teacher,
Mary, my angel from Angel and
Rowena and Kerry who took a chance
on me. I love them all greatly. Also,
special praise to my Kitty Belle, who
has become essential to Bob and me.

Contents

*There is something about the presence of
a cat . . . that seems to take the bite out of
being alone.*

Louis Camuti

*If man could be crossed with the cat, it
would improve man but deteriorate the
cat.*

Mark Twain

Chapter 1
A Bad Start

Our bad day began when my alarm failed to go off. I'd overslept.

'Bob!' I gasped. 'We're going to be late!'

Bob looked at me with his big green eyes.

Chill out, James, he seemed to say. *We have this under control.*

I wrapped an extra-thick scarf around

Bob's neck to keep out the chill then I grabbed my stuff. We dashed out of my flat in Tottenham, north London, heading for the bus that would take us to Islington, where I sold the homeless magazine *The Big Issue*. Bob ran beside me. We leaped on to the bus with moments to spare.

'We made it!' I said in relief.

But barely five minutes into our journey, things went from bad to worse.

Bob was in his usual position, half asleep on the seat next to me, when he suddenly lifted his head, looking around suspiciously.

I smell trouble, his body language said.

In the two years since I'd met him, Bob was usually right. Today was no exception. Within moments the bus was filled with an acrid, burning smell.

'This journey is terminating here,' said the panicked driver over the speaker. 'Everyone off the bus. Immediately!'

It wasn't quite the evacuation of the *Titanic*, but the bus was three quarters full so there was a lot of chaotic pushing and jostling. Bob didn't seem in a rush. Deciding to trust him, I left the others to it. So Bob and I were among the last to get off. As it turned out, that was a wise decision. The bus may have smelled awful but at least it was warm.

We had stopped opposite a new building site. Icy winds were whipping towards us through the site at a rate of knots. I was glad that I'd wrapped the extra-thick, woollen scarf around Bob's neck that morning.

'It's just an overheated engine,' the driver informed us after a few minutes.

'We have to wait for a bus company mechanic to fix it.'

So, amid much grumbling and complaining, about two dozen of us were left standing on the freezing cold pavement for almost half an hour while we waited for a replacement bus.

By the time Bob and I hopped off at our destination, Islington Green, we had been on the road for more than an hour and a half. We were now seriously late. I was going to miss the lunchtime rush, one of the best times for selling the magazine.

As usual, the five-minute walk to Angel tube station was a stop-start affair. It always was when I had Bob with me. Sometimes I walked with him on a leather lead, but more often than not he perched on my shoulders, gazing curiously out at the world, like the look-out on the prow of a ship. It wasn't something people were used to seeing every day of the week, so we could never walk more than ten yards without someone wanting to say hello and stroke him, or take a photograph. That didn't bother me at all. I knew Bob relished the attention.

The first person to stop us today was a little Russian lady.

'Oh, *koschka*, so pretty!' she said.

I stopped to let her say hello properly, but she immediately reached up to Bob and tried to touch him on the nose. Not a clever move.

Bob lashed out with a wild wave of his paw and a very loud *eeeeeow*. Fortunately he didn't scratch the lady, but he did leave her a little shaken. I had to spend a few minutes making sure she was all right.

'You should never do that to an animal, madam,' I told her, smiling and being as polite as possible. 'How would you react if someone tried to put their hands on your face? You're lucky he didn't scratch you.'

'I no mean to upset him,' she said. 'I very sorry, very sorry.'

I felt a bit sorry for her.

'Come on, you two, let's be friends,' I said.

Bob eventually allowed her to run her hand, very gently, along the back of his neck. The lady was very apologetic – and very hard to shake off.

When we finally got to the tube station, I put my rucksack on the pavement so that Bob could lie down on it – our regular routine. Then I started laying out my stack of *The Big Issue* magazines. I had to sell at least a couple of dozen today because, as usual, I needed the money.

But before I'd managed to sell a single magazine the heavens opened, raining down on me and Bob and forcing us to take shelter in an underpass near a bank and some office buildings.

Bob really hates the rain, especially when it's freezing cold. This day he almost seemed to shrink in it. His bright marmalade-coloured coat also seemed to turn a little bit greyer and less noticeable. Unsurprisingly, fewer people than usual stopped to make a fuss over him, so I sold fewer magazines than usual too.

Bob was soon making it clear that he didn't want to hang around. He kept shooting me withering looks and, like some kind of ginger hedgehog, scrunched himself up into a ball.

'I get the message, Bob,' I sighed. 'But it's nearly the weekend and I need to make enough money to keep us both going. My stack of magazines is still as thick as when we arrived. We have to sell some!'

Chapter 2
The Night Watchman

The weather wasn't improving. Then, midway through the afternoon, a young, uniformed police officer approached us.

'Are you supposed to be selling those magazines here, sir?' he said.

'I am perfectly entitled to sell magazines here, officer,' I said politely. 'I have my registered vendor ID and, unless I am causing a public nuisance, I can sell magazines at this spot from dawn 'til dusk.'

He looked unconvinced. 'Turn out your pockets, sir,' he said. 'Let's see what you've got.'

I had no idea what he was frisking me for but he didn't find anything.

'This cat yours, sir?' he asked, turning his attention to Bob now.

'Yes, officer,' I said. 'He is legally registered to me and microchipped.'

That seemed to worsen his mood. He walked off with a look almost as grim as the weather.

By early evening, I decided to call it quits. I felt deflated. I'd barely sold ten magazines and made only a fraction of what I'd normally expect to make. I'd spent long enough living off tins of reduced price beans and even cheaper loaves of bread to know that I wouldn't starve. I had enough money to top up the gas and electric meters and buy a meal or two for Bob as well. But it meant I'd probably need to head out to work again over the weekend. I really didn't want to do that. More rain was forecast, and I was starting to feel under the weather myself.

On the bus home, I could feel the first signs of flu seeping into my bones. I was aching and having hot flushes.

That's all I need, I thought, easing myself deep into my bus seat and settling down for a nap.

By now the sky had turned an inky black and the streetlights were on full blaze. There was something about London at night that fascinated Bob. As I drifted in and out of sleep, he sat beside me staring out of the bus window, lost in his own world.

Somewhere past Newington Green, I must have dropped off to sleep completely. I was woken by something lightly tapping me on the leg and the feeling of whiskers brushing against my cheek. I opened my eyes to see Bob with his face close to mine, patting me on the knee with his paw.

'What is it?' I said, slightly grumpily.

He started making a move off the seat towards the aisle, throwing me slightly concerned glances as he did so.

Are you coming or not? he seemed to say.

I looked out on to the street and realised where we were – right by where we needed to get off! Grabbing my rucksack, I hit the stop button just in the nick of time. If it hadn't been for my little night watchman, we'd have flown past our bus stop.

On the way home I popped into the convenience store on the corner of our road and bought myself some cheap flu remedy tablets. I also got Bob some nibbles and a pouch of his favourite chicken dinner. It was the least I could do. It had been a miserable day and it would have been easy to feel sorry for myself. But, back in the warmth of my little, one-bedroomed flat, I realised something.

'I have no real cause to complain, do I, Bob?' I said, watching him wolfing down his food. 'If I'd stayed asleep on the bus much longer I could easily have ended up miles away.'

Looking out of the window, I could see that the weather was getting worse. If I'd been out in this rain, I could easily have developed something a lot worse than mild flu. I'd had a fortunate escape.

I was lucky in more ways than one. There's an old saying I know: *A wise man doesn't grieve for the things he doesn't have, but is grateful for the good things that he does have.*

After dinner, I sat on the sofa, wrapped in a blanket and sipping a hot drink. I looked at Bob snoozing contentedly in his favourite spot near the radiator. To him, our earlier troubles were long forgotten. In that moment he couldn't have been happier.

'I should view the world the same way,' I told myself. After all, there were so many good things I was grateful for at this moment in my life. Not least of them, Bob himself.

It was now a little over two years since I had found Bob, lying injured on the ground floor of this same block of flats. When I spotted him in the dingy light of the hallway, he looked like he'd been attacked by another animal. He had wounds on the back of his legs and on his body.

At first I thought he belonged to someone else. But after seeing him in the same place for a few days, I took him up to my flat and nursed him back to health. I had to fork out almost every penny I had to buy him medicine, but it was worth it. We formed an instant bond.

Bob appeared to be a stray so I assumed that he'd return to the streets. But he refused to leave my side. Each day I'd put him outside and try to send him on his way, and each day he'd follow

me down the road or pop up in the hallway in the evening, inviting himself in
for the night.

They say that cats choose you, not the
other way round. I realised Bob had
chosen me when he followed me to the
bus stop a mile from home. When I
shooed him away and watched him disappear into the busy crowds, I thought
that was the last I'd see of him. But as
the bus was pulling away, Bob appeared
out of nowhere, leaping on board in a
blur of ginger, plonking himself down on
the seat next to me. And that had been
that.

Bob and I were kindred spirits,
helping each other to heal the wounds
of our troubled pasts. I gave Bob companionship, food and somewhere warm
to lay his head at night. In return he

gave me a new hope and purpose in life. He gave me loyalty, love and humour, and a sense of responsibility I'd never felt before. He also gave me some goals and helped me see the world more clearly than I had done for a long, long time.

For more than a decade I'd been a drug addict, sleeping rough around London, oblivious to the world around me.

As a homeless person, I was invisible. I forgot how to function and how to interact with people. In a way I was dead to the world. But now, with Bob's help, I was slowly coming back to life. I was still on medication, but could see the light at the end of the tunnel. I hoped to be completely drug-free soon.

It wasn't easy. It never is for a recovering addict. Working on the streets didn't help. Trouble was always around the corner, and I had a knack for attracting it. I longed to get off the streets and put that life behind me. I had no idea when or how that was going to be possible but, with Bob beside me, I was determined to try.

By most people's standards, I still didn't have much. I never had a lot of money and I didn't live in a flashy apartment or have a car. But I had my flat and my job selling *The Big Issue*. For the first time in years, I was heading in the right direction – with Bob to offer me friendship and to guide me on my way.

As I picked myself up and headed to bed for an early night, I leaned over and gave Bob a gentle ruffle on the back of his neck.

'Where would I be without you, little fella?'

Chapter 3
New Tricks

Some people start their mornings listening to the radio, others with their exercises or a cup of tea or coffee. Bob and I start ours by playing games together.

The moment I wake up, Bob shuffles out of his bed in the corner of the bedroom, walks over and starts staring at me. Soon after that he starts making a chirruping noise, a bit like a phone.

Brr, brr.

If that doesn't get my full attention, he starts making another noise, slightly more plaintive and pleading.

Waaaah. Waaaah!

Sometimes he places his paws on the side of the mattress and hauls himself up so that he is almost at eye-level with me. He then dabs a paw in my direction.

Don't ignore me! he seems to say. *I've been awake for ages and I'm hungry, so where's my breakfast?*

If I am too slow to respond, he steps up the charm offensive and does what I call a 'Puss in Boots', like the character in the *Shrek* movies, and stares wide-eyed at me with his piercing green eyes. It is heartbreakingly cute and totally irresistible. It always makes me smile. And it always works.

I always keep a packet of Bob's favourite snacks in a drawer by the side of the bed. Depending on how I am feeling, I might let him come up on the bed for a cuddle and a couple of treats. Or, if I am in a more playful mood, I'll throw them around the room for him to chase. Bob often catches the treats in mid-flight, like a cricketer or baseball player fielding a ball. He leaps up and catches them in his paws. He has even caught them in his mouth a couple of times. It's amazing to watch.

On other occasions, he'll entertain himself. One hot summer's morning, for instance, Bob was curled up in a shady spot in the bedroom fast asleep. Or so I thought.

Suddenly he sat up and jumped on the bed. Using it as a trampoline, he bounced himself at the wall behind my head, hitting it quite hard with his paws.

'Bob, what the — ?' I said, gobsmacked.

I looked at the duvet and saw a little millipede lying there. Bob was eyeing it, clearly ready to crunch it in his mouth.

'Oh no you don't, mate,' I said, knowing that insects can be poisonous to cats. 'You don't know where that's been.'

He shot me a look. *Spoilsport*, he seemed to say.

I have always been amazed at Bob's speed, strength and athleticism. Someone suggested to me once that he must be related to a lynx or some kind of wild cat. It is entirely possible. Bob's past is a complete mystery to me. I don't know how old he is and I know nothing about the life he led before I found him. Unless I do a DNA test on him, I'll never know where he comes from or who his parents were. To be honest though, I don't really care. Bob is Bob. And that is all I need to know.

I am not the only one who's learned to love Bob for being his colourful, unpredictable self.

In the spring of 2009, we had been selling *The Big Issue* for a year or so, and Bob had built up a small but dedicated band of admirers at our pitch outside the Angel Islington tube station.

As far as I knew, we were the only human/feline team selling *The Big Issue* in London. But even if there was another one, I suspected the feline part of the partnership wasn't much competition for Bob when it came to drawing – and pleasing – a crowd.

During our early days together, when I had been a busker in Covent Garden playing the guitar and singing, Bob had just sat there, Buddha-like, watching the world going about its business. People were fascinated by him and would stop, stroke and talk to him.

'What's your story?' they would ask. 'How did you guys meet?'

And I'd tell them. But that was about the extent of it.

Since we'd been selling *The Big Issue*, however, we'd developed a few tricks.

Bob loved to play, so I'd bring along little toys that he would toss around and chase. His favourite was a little grey mouse that had once been filled with catnip.

The mouse had lost its catnip a long time ago. Its stitching was coming apart and, although it had always been grey, it had now become a really dirty shade of grey. Bob had loads of other toys but 'Scraggedy Mouse', as I called it, was his number one toy.

He would hold it in his mouth, flicking it from side to side. Sometimes he'd whirl it around by its tail and release it so that it flew a couple of feet away. Then he'd pounce on it and start the whole process again. Bob loved hunting real mice, so he was obviously mimicking that. It always stopped people in their tracks. I'd known commuters to spend ten minutes standing there, hypnotised by Bob and his game.

Soon I started playing too. To begin with, Bob and I just played at shaking hands. I'd stretch out my hand and Bob would extend his paw to hold it. We were only doing what we did at home in my flat but people seemed to find it sweet. If I had a pound for every time someone – usually a lady – stopped and said something like, 'Aah, how sweet!' or 'That's adorable!' I'd be rich.

My playtimes with Bob became more than simple entertainment for the passing crowds. It helped me to pass the time, to keep warm on the freezing street and to enjoy my days a little more too. It also encouraged people to buy copies of the magazine. It was another one of the blessings that Bob had bestowed on me.

We began to develop our act a little further.

Bob loved his little treats. For instance,

if I held a cat biscuit three feet or so above him, he'd stand on his hind legs in an effort to snaffle the snack from my hand. He would wrap his paws around my wrist to steady himself, then let go with one paw and try to grab it.

This went down a storm. So we developed the trick even more. Bob's grip when he grabbed my arm to reach the treat was as strong as a vice. So every now and again I would slowly and very gently raise him in the air so that he was dangling a few inches above the ground. He would hang there for a few seconds until he let go, or I eased him back to earth. I always made sure he had a soft landing of course, and usually put my rucksack under him.

The more of a show we put on, the more people seemed to respond to us.

They became more generous too and not just in buying *The Big Issue*.

Since our early days, people had been incredibly kind, giving us cat snacks and nibbles. They had also started giving us items of clothing, often hand-knitted or sewn by them. Bob now had a collection of scarves in all sorts of colours, and I was running out of space to keep them all. It was a little overwhelming at times to receive such warmth, support and love.

But those who felt very differently about us were never very far away . . .

Chapter 4
A Tough Customer

It was the Friday evening rush hour, and the crowds passing in and out of Angel tube station were growing thicker by the minute. Bob was totally oblivious to the commotion, flapping his tail absent-mindedly from side to side as he lay on my rucksack on the pavement.

I suddenly noticed a lady standing a

few feet away from us. She was staring intently at Bob.

From the way she was muttering and shaking her head, I sensed she disapproved of us. I didn't plan on talking to her, mainly because I was too busy trying to sell the last few copies of the magazine before the weekend. Unfortunately, she had other ideas.

'Young man. Can't you see that this cat is in distress?' she said, approaching us.

She looked like a headmistress: middle-aged with a cut-glass English accent and wearing a tweed skirt and jacket. But she was much more aggressive than any teacher I remember.

'I have been watching you for a while and I can see that your cat is wagging its tail,' she said. 'That means it's not happy.

You shouldn't be exploiting it like this. You aren't fit to look after it.'

We'd heard this a lot since Bob and I had started working the streets together. I politely defended myself from the lady's accusations.

'He's wagging his tail because he's content. If he didn't want to be here, madam, you wouldn't see him for dust. He's a cat. They choose who they want to be with. He's free to run off whenever he wants.'

'So why is he on a lead?' she shot back, a smug look on her face.

'He's only on a lead here and when we are on the streets,' I explained. 'He ran off once and was terrified when he couldn't find me again. I let him off when he goes to do his business. So, again, if he wasn't happy, as you claim, he'd be gone the minute I took the lead off, wouldn't he?'

This lady was having none of it.

'No, no, no. It's a well-known fact that if a cat is wagging its tail it is a distress signal,' she said, more animated now.

Bob had begun backing towards me, ready to jump into my arms if things got out of hand. I tried to ease the lady's fears by telling her a little about us.

'We've been together for more than two years. He wouldn't have been with me two minutes if I was mistreating him,' I said.

But whatever I said, she just shook her head and tutted away.

'Why don't we agree to differ?' I said at last.

'*Hffff*,' she said, waving her arms at me. 'I'm not agreeing with anything you say, young man.'

To my huge relief, she started walking

away into the crowds jostling around the entrance to the tube station.

I was soon distracted by a couple of customers. Their smiles were a welcome relief. I was handing one of them their change when I heard a noise behind me that I recognised immediately.

Wheeeeeow! Bob yowled.

I spun round. Not only had the woman in the tweed suit come back, she was now holding Bob in her arms. She held him awkwardly, one hand under his stomach and another on his back, as if she'd never picked up an animal before. She could have been holding a joint of meat that she'd just bought at the butcher.

Bob was clearly furious and was wriggling like crazy.

'What do you think you are doing?' I

shouted. 'Put him down or I'll call the police!'

'He needs to be taken somewhere safe,' she said, a slightly crazed expression on her face.

She was going to run off with him! I prepared to drop my supply of magazines and chase her through the streets of Islington.

Luckily, Bob's long lead was still tethered to my rucksack. For a moment there was a kind of stand-off. But then I saw her eye moving along the lead to the rucksack.

'No you don't,' I said, stepping forward to intercept her.

My movement caught her off guard. This gave Bob his chance.

Wheeeeow! he screeched again and freed himself from the woman's grip. He didn't scratch her, but he did dig his paws into her arm which forced her to drop him on to the pavement.

He landed with a bit of a bump, then stood there growling and hissing and baring his teeth at her. I'd never seen him so aggressive.

Unbelievably, the lady used this as an argument against me.

'See? He's angry,' she said, addressing the watching crowd.

'He's angry because you just picked him up without his permission,' I said. 'He only lets me pick him up.'

'No, he's angry because of the way you are treating him,' she insisted. 'Everyone can see that. That's why he should be taken away from you. He doesn't want to be with you.'

Everyone held their breath to see what

happened next. It was Bob who broke the silence.

He gave the woman a really disdainful look, then padded his way back towards me. He began rubbing his head against the outside of my leg, and purring noisily when I put my hand down to stroke him.

He then plonked his rear down on the ground and looked up at me playfully.

Now can we get on with some more tricks? he seemed to say.

I dipped my hand into my coat pocket and produced a treat. Almost immediately, Bob got up on his hind legs and grabbed hold of my arm. I then popped the treat into his mouth drawing a couple of audible *aaahs* from somewhere behind me.

Bob had played to the crowd perfectly. It was as if he was saying: *I'm with James, and I'm really happy to be with James. And anyone who says otherwise is mistaken. End of story.*

Most of the onlookers got the message. They turned to the woman in the tweed suit.

'We know this guy, he's cool,' one young man in a business suit said.

'Yes, leave them alone. They're not doing anyone any harm and he looks after his cat really well,' another middle-aged lady said.

One or two other people made supportive noises. Not one person backed up the lady in the tweed suit. She spluttered and grumbled for a moment or two, but realised that she had lost the battle. So she disappeared once more into the crowds, this time – thankfully – permanently.

'You OK, James?' one of the onlookers asked me, as I kneeled down to check
on Bob. He was purring loudly, but his
breathing was steady and there was no
sign of any injury from when he was
dropped to the ground.

'I'm fine, thanks,' I muttered, not
being entirely honest.

I hated it when people implied I was using Bob. It hurt me deeply. Bob wanted to be with me. He'd proven that time and time again. Unfortunately, that meant that he had to spend his days with me on the streets. Those were the simple facts of my life. I didn't have a choice.

This made us easy targets. Most people judged us kindly. I had learned to accept that there would always be those who would not.

Chapter 5
The Bobmobile

It was a balmy, early summer afternoon and I decided to stop work early. The sunny weather had put a smile on everyone's face and I'd sold out my supply of magazines in a few hours.

Before I caught the bus home, I decided to buy some more magazines for the rest of the week. With Bob on my shoulders, I headed over to see Rita, the co-ordinator for *The Big Issue*, on the north side of Islington High Street.

From a distance, I could see that she and a group of vendors in red bibs were huddled around something. It turned out to be a bicycle.

'What's this, Rita?' I joked. 'Riding in the Tour de France?'

'Don't think so, James,' she smiled. 'Someone just sold it to me in exchange for ten magazines. I don't know what to do with it.'

The bike wasn't in prime condition. There was rust on the handlebars and the light at the front had cracked glass. The paintwork had a few chips and nicks and, just for good measure, one of the mudguards had been snapped in half.

'Is it roadworthy?' I asked Rita.

'I think so,' she said. 'Apart from the front brakes needing a bit of attention.'

I stared at the bike. I was no Bradley Wiggins, but I had ridden bikes throughout my childhood and again in London. And I knew a bit about cycle maintenance.

'Why don't you give it a try?' Rita suggested, seeing the look in my eye.

'Why not?' I said. 'Can you keep an eye on Bob for a second?'

Handing Bob's lead to Rita, I took the bike and flipped it upside down to inspect it properly. The tyres were inflated and the chain looked like it was well oiled and moving pretty freely. The seat was a little low for me, so I adjusted it. Then I climbed on.

Bob was soaking up the sunshine on the pavement near Rita but kept half an eye on me throughout. He tilted his head to one side slightly, as if to say: *What's that thing and why are you sitting on top of it?*

'Bear with me, Bob,' I told him, as I gave the bike a quick spin.

The gears were a tad on the sticky side and, as Rita had warned me, the front brakes weren't working properly. I figured there was a problem with the wire inside the cable, which was easily fixed. The rear brakes were fine, however, which was all I needed to know.

'I'll give you a tenner for it, Rita,' I said, bringing the bike back.

'Deal,' said Rita, a little taken aback. 'You'll need this as well.'

She fished around under her trolley of magazines and produced a rather battered, old black cycle helmet.

The bike was one of the first, sensible investments I'd made in a while. I knew it would be useful back home in Tottenham, where I could use it for short journeys to the shops or the doctor's. I'd make the £10 back in saved bus fares in no time. For the longer journey to work, I'd carry on taking the bus or the tube. That journey was too treacherous to cycle, and full of notorious cycling accident spots.

Then something struck me. How was I going to get it home? Bus drivers don't let bikes on board, and there was no prospect of getting it on a tube.

There's only one thing for it, I told myself.

'OK, Bob, looks like you and I are riding this home,' I said.

He looked suspiciously at me again as I strapped on the cycle helmet, slung my rucksack on my shoulders and started wheeling the bike towards him.

'Come on, mate, climb on board,' I said, reaching down to him and letting him climb on my shoulders.

'Good luck,' Rita said.

'Thanks. I think we'll need it!' I said.

I walked the bike along the pavement for a while, towards Islington Memorial Green. We passed a couple of police officers who gave us a curious look, but said nothing. There was no law against riding a bike with a cat on your shoulders after all.

The looks on people's faces ranged from astonishment to hilarity. More than one person stopped in their tracks, pointing at us as if we were visitors from another planet.

When we reached the Green, we cut

across the corner past Waterstones bookshop and turned into Essex Road, the main road to north London.

'Here we go, Bob,' I said, bracing myself to enter the heavy traffic.

We started weaving our way through the buses, vans, cars and lorries. Bob and I soon got the hang of it. As I focused on staying upright, Bob decided, sensibly, to drape himself across my neck with his head down low and pointing forward. He clearly wanted to settle down and enjoy the ride.

It was mid-afternoon and a lot of children were heading home from school. All along Essex Road, groups of kids in uniforms stopped and waved at us. I tried waving back at one point but lost my balance a little bit, sending Bob sliding down my shoulder.

'Oops, sorry, mate. Won't do that again,' I said.

Progress was steady but slow at times. If we had to stop because of traffic, we were instantly shouted at by someone asking for a photo. At one point, two teenage schoolgirls jumped out into the road to snap themselves with us.

'This is so cute!' one of them said, leaning into us so heavily as she posed for her photo that she almost knocked us over.

I hadn't ridden a bicycle for a few years, and I wasn't exactly in prime physical condition, so I took a little breather every now and again, attracting a posse of onlookers each time I did so. Most smiled their approval but a couple shook their heads.

'Stupid idiot,' I heard one middle-aged guy in a suit say as he strode past us.

It didn't feel stupid at all. In fact, it felt rather fun. And I could tell Bob was having a good time too. His head was right next to mine and I could feel him purring contentedly in my ear.

I had been looking forward to the section of our journey where we headed towards Seven Sisters. At that point, the road dropped downhill for a mile or so. I'd be able to freewheel down it quite easily.

To my delight, there was a dedicated bike lane, which was completely empty. Bob and I were soon flying down the hill, the warm summer air blowing through our hair. We must have been going close to twenty miles per hour at one point.

'Woohoo! Isn't this great, Bob?' I said happily.

The traffic in the main lane to our right was gridlocked, and people were winding down their windows to let in some air. Some of the expressions on their faces as we whizzed past them were priceless.

A couple of children stuck their heads out of the sun-roofs of their cars and shouted at us. A few people just looked on in utter disbelief. That was under-standable. You don't see a ginger cat whizzing down a hill on a bike very often.

It only took me about half an hour to get home. Pretty impressive, consider-ing we'd had so many unplanned stops.

As we pulled up outside my block of flats, Bob just hopped off my shoulders like he'd been riding the bus. He had taken it all in his stride as just another routine day in London.

Back in the flat, I spent the rest of the afternoon and evening tinkering with the bike. I'd soon fixed the front brakes and given it a general tuning up.

'There you go,' I said to Bob, as I stood back to admire my handiwork. 'I think we've got ourselves a Bobmobile.'

I was pretty sure that the look he gave me signalled his approval.

Chapter 6
Body Language

People often ask me how Bob and I communicate with each other so well.

'It's simple,' I say. 'He has his own language, and I've learned to understand it.'

It might sound far-fetched but it's true.

Bob mainly uses body language. For instance, if he wants to go to the toilet when we are walking around the streets, he starts grumbling and growling. He then starts fidgeting on my shoulders. I don't need to look at him to know what he is up to. He's scouting around for a spot with some soft dirt where he can do his business.

If he is walking on his lead and gets tired, he lets out a light, low-pitched grumble or moan-cum-growl and refuses to walk another inch. He just looks at me as if to say, *Come on, mate, pick me up, I'm worn out.*

If he ever gets scared, he backs up on my shoulders. If he gets scared when he is standing on the ground, he reverses between my legs in case I need to pick him up. It is rare that anything frightens him though. Living and working in central London means the sound of an ambulance or a police car going by with their sirens blaring barely bothers him at all. The only thing that freaks him a little is the pressurised air brakes on big lorries and buses. Whenever he hears that loud, hissing sound, he recoils and looks scared. On bonfire nights, he also gets a little nervous about the loud bangs and explosions, but he generally enjoys watching the bright, sparkling lights in the sky from the window of my flat.

I can tell a lot about his mood from the way he moves his tail. If he is snoozing or asleep, his tail is still and quiet, of course. But at other times he wags it around. The most common wag is a gentle side-to-side movement, rather like a windscreen wiper on its slowest setting. This is his contentment wag. I've spent endless hours sitting around London with him and have seen him doing it when he is entertained or intrigued by something. The lady who tried to steal him at Angel wasn't the first person to misread this as a sign of anger. Bob does get angry but he signals that with a very different tail movement where he flicks it around, a bit like a fly swatter.

There are subtler messages too. If, for instance, he is worried about me, he comes up really close. If I am feeling ill, he often sidles up and listens to my chest. He does a lot of loving things like that. He has this habit of rubbing against me, purring. He also rubs his face on my hand, tilting his head so that I can scratch behind his ear. Animal behaviourists and zoologists are entitled to their opinions but, to me, this is Bob's way of telling me that he loves me.

Of course, his favourite subject is food. If he wants me to come to the kitchen to feed him, for instance, he goes around banging on the doors. He is so clever; he could easily unpick the child locks I've fitted on my food cupboards to keep him out, so I always have to go and check. By the time I get there, he has always moved to a spot by the radiator in the corner where he'll be wearing his most innocent look.

For a while, his biggest challenge was getting my attention while I played on the second-hand Xbox I'd picked up in a charity shop.

Bob was fascinated by certain video games, especially motor racing ones. On one occasion, I could have sworn I saw his body swaying as we took a particularly sharp hairpin bend together. He drew the line at action games with a lot of shooting, however. If I was playing one of these, he would head for another corner of the room. If the game – or I – ever got too loud, he'd lift up his head and look across. The message was simple: *Turn it down, please. I'm trying to snooze.*

Sometimes I could get really wrapped up in a game. Bob didn't appreciate this, especially when he was hungry, so he took more drastic measures.

I was playing a game with my friend Belle one night when Bob appeared. He'd had dinner a couple of hours earlier and had decided that he needed a snack. He went through his usual attention-seeking routine, making a selection of noises, draping himself across my feet

57

and rubbing himself against my legs. But we were both so heavily involved in reaching the next level of our game that we didn't respond at all.

He sloped off, circling the area where the TV and Xbox were plugged in. After a moment, he moved in towards the control console and pressed his head against the big, touch-sensitive button in the middle.

'Bob, what are you up to?' I asked, still too engrossed in the game to twig what he was doing.

A moment later, the screen went black and the Xbox started powering down. Bob had applied enough pressure to the button to switch it off. We had been halfway through a really tricky level of the game, so we should have been furious with him. But we both sat there with the same expression of disbelief on our faces.

'Did he just do what I think he did?' Belle asked me.

Bob stood there looking triumphant. His expression said it all.

Let's see you try and ignore me now.

We don't always rely on signals and body language. There are times when we have a strange kind of telepathy. We've also learned to alert each other to danger.

A few days after I'd acquired the bike, I decided to take Bob to a local park. By now he was completely comfortable riding around on my shoulders, leaning in and out of the corners like a motorbike pillion rider.

In the park, Bob was keen to explore. When I felt it was safe, I let him off his lead so that he could enjoy himself in the undergrowth while he did his business. I was sitting, reading a comic and soaking up a few rays of sunshine when, in the distance, I heard the barking of a dog.

Uh oh, I thought.

A very large, menacing German shepherd was running towards the park entrance. The dog was no more than a hundred and fifty yards away and was off its leash. I could tell it was looking for trouble.

'Bob!' I shouted at the undergrowth. 'Bob, come here!'

Bob understood what was happening immediately and bolted out of the bushes. He wasn't afraid of dogs but he picked his battles wisely. This wasn't a dog to pick a fight with.

Bob's bright ginger coat wasn't exactly hard to spot. I saw the dog accelerate towards us, barking even more fiercely. I had a terrible feeling that Bob had left it too late, so I grabbed the bike and got ready to ride it into the firing line if necessary. If the German shepherd intercepted him, Bob could be in serious trouble.

As so often in the past, however, I'd underestimated him.

He sprinted across the grass as I crouched down on one knee. In one seamless move, I flipped him on to my shoulders, jumped straight on to the bike and – with Bob standing on my shoulders – hit the pedals and began cycling out of the park.

The frustrated German shepherd

pursued us for a short time as we sped down the street. Bob was hissing at him. I couldn't see Bob's face, but it wouldn't have surprised me at all if he was taunting him.

What are you going to do about it now, tough guy? he was probably saying.

'That was a close one, Bob,' I said when at last we got clear. 'Thank goodness for the Bobmobile.'

Chapter 7
The Odd Couple

The intercom buzzer went just after 9am one weekday morning as Bob and I got ready for work.

'Who the heck is that?' I said, instinctively twitching at the curtains for a look even though I had no view of the entrance from up on the fifth floor.

'James, it's Titch. Can I come up with

Princess?' a familiar voice said over the speaker.

Titch was a tiny wiry bloke with short, thinning hair. Like me, he was a recovering addict who had started selling *The Big Issue.* He had been having a hard time lately, and had been 'de-badged' and given a six-month suspension for not showing up at work enough. I knew he was struggling to make ends meet.

I felt like I'd been given a second chance in life since I'd met Bob so I'd given Titch another opportunity as well. I also quite liked him. Deep down, I knew he had a good heart.

Another reason that Titch and I got on was that we both worked on the street with our pet as our companion. In Titch's case it was his sweet-natured black Labrador-Staffordshire bull terrier-cross,

Princess. Princess and Bob had never met though I braced myself for what might happen when Titch and Princess arrived at the front door.

When Bob saw Princess, he arched his back and hissed. Cats arch their backs to make themselves look bigger in a fight. They also make their fur stand on end for the same reason.

The moment Princess saw Bob in full, confrontational mode she froze to the spot.

'It's all right, Princess,' I said. 'Bob won't hurt you.'

I then led her into my bedroom and shut the door so that she felt safe.

'James, mate. Is there any way you can look after Princess for the day?' Titch said, cutting straight to the chase. 'I've got to sort something out.'

'Sure,' I said. 'Shouldn't be a problem. Should it, Bob?'

Bob gave me an enigmatic look.

'We are working at Angel today. Princess will be all right with us there, won't she?' I said.

'Yeah, no problem,' Titch said. 'So how about if I pick her up there this evening at about 6pm?'

It was all fixed.

'Be a good girl, Princess,' Titch said before heading off.

Bob didn't have a problem with dogs unless they were aggressive towards him so I wasn't worried about him. In our early days busking around Covent Garden, I'd seen him give one dog a bop on the nose with his paw.

Dogs were one thing. Cats were another. There were times when I wondered whether Bob knew he *was* a cat. He seemed to think they were inferior beings, unfit to breathe the same air as him. When money was tight, we'd walk to Angel rather than take the bus, and Bob would sniff and stare whenever we went past what was clearly a house that had cats inside.

If he ever saw another cat out and about he would let them know in no uncertain terms that this was his turf. Once, when he saw a tabby cat skulking around on Islington Green, Bob had strained so hard to get at the upstart invading his territory that it was like having an aggressive dog on the end of the lead. He had to stamp his authority on the situation. Obviously, he'd done the same with Princess.

I was a little worried that having

Princess that day would be a bit of an inconvenience. Dogs were much more hard work than cats. For a start, you couldn't put them on your shoulders as you walked down the street. It was a design flaw that, I soon discovered, slowed you down considerably.

Walking to the bus stop, Princess pulled on the lead, stopped to sniff random patches of grass and veered off to go to the toilet three times in the space of a couple of hundred yards.

'Come on, Princess, or we'll never get there,' I said, already regretting my decision.

On the bus, Bob took up his normal position on the seat next to the window and kept a watchful eye on Princess, who was tucked under my feet. The looks he gave Princess whenever she moved into his territory during the journey were hilarious. The area under the seat wasn't exactly spacious and Princess would occasionally wiggle to improve her position. Each time she did so, Bob gave her a look that said, *Sit still, you stupid dog.*

Outside the weather was atrocious, with rain hammering down. I took Bob to the little park at Islington Green to quickly do his business and decided to let Princess do the same. Big mistake. She took forever to find a suitable spot. I'd forgotten to bring any plastic bags with me so had to fish around in a rubbish bin to find something with which to scoop everything up. I really wasn't enjoying my day as a dog sitter.

With the rain getting heavier by the minute, I took shelter under the canopy of a café.

'Can I get a cup of tea, please?' I asked when a waitress appeared. 'And a saucer of milk for my cat and some water for the dog?'

The waitress smiled, like she served cats and dogs every day. 'Sure,' she said.

I then popped inside to use the toilet, leaving my two companions tied to the table with their leads.

When I got back, their positions had changed. I'd left them with Bob on a chair and Princess under the table. Now Bob was sitting on the table, lapping at his saucer of milk, while Princess was under the table looking far from happy with her bowl of water. Bob was top dog once again.

Despite the weather, Bob was still attracting attention from passers-by.

'Hello,' cooed a couple of ladies, stopping and stroking him.

It was as if poor Princess wasn't even there. I knew how she felt. I live in Bob's shadow sometimes.

But in the end, Princess proved very useful. She sat there, her eyes swivelling around like cameras, checking out everyone who approached us. If she liked the look of them, she stayed where she was. But if she didn't, she suddenly sat upright, and let out a little growl or even a bark. It was usually enough to get the message across.

If anyone knelt down to stroke and say hello to Bob, Princess would make sure that they were treating him with respect. She made my job a little easier.

It was often a challenge to keep an eye on Bob while trying to sell the magazine at the same time. The incident with the lady in the tweed suit had made me especially wary.

'Thank you, Princess,' I began saying, handing her a little treat from my rucksack.

Even Bob shot her a couple of approving looks. *Maybe she's not so bad after all*, he may have been thinking.

The weather remained miserable all afternoon, so when the clock started edging towards six, I started looking out for Titch. But 6pm came and went and there was no sign of him.

'Have you seen Titch?' I asked one of the *The Big Issue* co-ordinators.

'I haven't seen him for weeks,' she said, shaking her head.

By 6.30pm, I knew he wasn't coming.

'Come on, you two, let's head for home. Titch can collect you there, Princess,' I said, gathering all my stuff together.

I was a little worried. If Titch didn't come, how would Bob feel about having Princess for a sleepover? I imagined lots of barking, complaints from the neighbours and a sleepless night for me.

I bought Princess some dog food and doggie biscuits on the way home. As we all settled down to dinner in the kitchen, Bob put Princess in her place again. When she moved towards the bowl of water I'd laid out for her, Bob hissed and snarled loudly, forcing Princess to back off. He had to lap up his own bowl of milk first.

It didn't take them long to reach an agreement though. In fact, Bob allowed

Princess to clear out the remains of his dinner bowl.

I've seen it all now, I thought to myself. But I hadn't.

By 10pm I'd fallen asleep in front of the television. When I woke up, I saw something that made me wish I owned a video camera.

Bob and Princess were both splayed out on the carpet, snoozing quietly. Princess's head was barely a foot from Bob's nose. They looked like lifelong pals.

'Sleep well, guys,' I said with a grin.

I locked the front door, switched off the lights and headed off to bed, leaving them there.

The following morning, I was woken up by the sound of barking. It took me a moment to remember that I had a dog in the house.

'What's wrong, Princess?' I said, still half asleep.

Titch was at the door. From the look of his bleary face, he had slept rough.

'Really sorry to leave you in the lurch last night but something came up,' he said, apologetically.

I'd had nights like that myself, far too many of them.

'No problem,' I said.

Titch looked like he could do with something warm inside him.

'Do you want a cup of tea and some toast?' I asked.

Bob was lying next to the radiator, with Princess curled up a couple of feet away. The expression on Titch's face when he saw them was priceless.

'Look at those two,' I smiled. 'They get on like a house on fire now.'

'I can see it, but I can't quite believe it,' Titch said, munching on his toast. 'So would you mind looking after her again if I'm in the lurch?'

'Why not?' I said.

Chapter 8
The Garbage Inspector

We all have our obsessions in life. For Bob, it's packaging.

Bubble wrap offers endless entertainment. Who doesn't love popping the bubbles? Bob goes absolutely crazy with excitement whenever I let him play with a sheet of it. I always keep a watchful eye on him. Each time he pops a bit with his paw or mouth, he turns and gives me a look.

Did you hear that? he seems to say.

Wrapping paper is another fascination and he is also obsessed by the crispy, crunchy cellophane cereal comes in. He can spend half an hour rustling a ball of cellophane. Balls of scrunched-up aluminium kitchen foil have the same effect.

His absolute favourite, though, is cardboard boxes. If I ever walk past Bob with a cardboard box in my hand, he lunges at me as if to grab it. It doesn't matter whether it is a cereal box, a milk carton or a bigger box. He just bounds up, paddling his paws quickly.

Give me that, he seems to demand. *I want to play with it NOW*.

He also loves hiding in the bigger boxes. It's given me the heebie-jeebies on at least one occasion.

I don't let Bob wander out of our flat on his own and the windows are always closed to avoid him climbing out. I know cats can 'self-right' themselves in the air and we were 'only' five floors up, but I don't want to test his flying abilities! So when I couldn't find him in any of his usual spots one summer evening, I panicked slightly.

'Bob, Bob, where are you, mate?' I said.

I looked high and low, but there was no sign of him in my bedroom or in the kitchen or bathroom. Then it suddenly struck me. I'd put a box containing some hand-me-down clothes in the airing cupboard. Sure enough, I opened the cupboard to see a distinctive ginger shape deep in the middle of the box.

He did the same thing again not

long afterwards, with almost disastrous consequences.

Belle had come around to help me tidy the place up a bit.

'You have to chuck out some of this old tat,' she told me, looking around the flat at all the junk I'd collected over the years. I had lived there for a few years now and I like collecting things I found out and about.

So we organised a few cardboard boxes full of old books and maps and broken radios and toasters. We were going to throw some in the rubbish and take others to charity shops or the local recycling place.

Belle was taking one box down to the rubbish area outside the flats and was waiting for the lift to arrive when her box started jiggling around.

Aaargh! she screamed, more than a bit freaked out.

By the time I opened the door to see what the trouble was, she'd dropped the box and discovered Bob inside. He was pulling himself out from a collection of old books and magazines, where he'd curled up for a nap. It was a close shave – we almost threw him out with the rubbish!

Soon after that I made him a bed out of a cardboard box. I figured that if he slept in one, he might be less obsessed with them at other times. So I took one side off a box, then lined it with a little blanket.

'You're as snug as a bug in there, aren't you, Bob?' I told him when I saw him curled up inside.

He looked at me and purred. He loved it.

Bob was also deeply interested in the rubbish bin in the kitchen. Whenever I put something into the bin, he would get up on his hind legs and stick his nose in.

'What are you looking for, mate?' I would challenge him.

He would throw me a look as if to say, *That depends on what you're throwing in there. I haven't decided if I want to play with it or not.*

'I'll call you the garbage inspector, shall I?' I laughed.

I was just emerging from the bath one morning when I heard weird noises coming from the kitchen. I could make out a thin, metallic, scraping sound, as if something was being dragged around, together with a kind of low moaning.

'Bob, what are you up to now?' I said,

grabbing a towel to dry my hair as I went to investigate.

I couldn't help giggling at the sight that greeted me.

Bob was standing in the middle of the kitchen floor with an empty tin of cat food wedged on the top of his head. The tin was sitting at a jaunty angle on his head, right over his eyes.

It was obvious that he couldn't see much, because he was walking backwards across the kitchen floor, dragging the tin with him as he tried to reverse out of it. He was being very deliberate, occasionally wiggling the tin or raising it a little before giving it a tap against the floor in the hope the impact would knock it off his head. His plan wasn't working. It was comical to watch.

In the corner of the room I could see

the black bin liner containing the rubbish I was going to put in the wheelie bins downstairs that morning. I normally emptied the bin and put the sack out at night, to stop Bob playing with it. But today I'd forgotten and left it on the kitchen floor. Big mistake.

Bob had ripped and chewed at the bottom of the bag to investigate what was inside. No cardboard boxes but he *had* found the old tin – and got his head stuck inside. What a mess.

Wrow, he meowed. It was a sad and pathetic little sound.

The tin had a serrated edge where it had been opened, so I was careful in removing it from his head. It was pretty stinky, that was for sure.

The moment he was free, Bob scooted off into the corner. There were bits of food stuck to his ear and the back of his head, so he began licking and washing himself frantically, shooting me sheepish looks.

It wasn't the first time he'd done something like this. One day I heard another odd sound coming from the kitchen, a kind of tapping sound. *Pat . . . pat . . . pat* followed by a faster *pat, pat, pat, pat.*

Bob had been walking around with a miniature container of butter attached to one of his paws. He loved butter and had been dipping his paw inside the container so that he could lick it clean. He'd somehow wedged his paw inside and was now walking around with it on his foot. Every now and again, he'd raise his paw and tap it against a cupboard door in an effort to shift it. Eventually I'd had to help.

'Bob, you silly boy. What have you done to yourself?' I said, leaning down to help him again.

Yes, he seemed to say, *I know it was a dumb thing to do. Don't tell me you've never done anything stupid yourself.*

Chapter 9
Worms

Even though money was tight, I always tried to feed him good food in the recommended portions. In the morning, Bob had a flat teacup full of high-nutrition biscuits. And at the end of the day, about an hour before he went to bed, he'd have half a teacup of biscuits and half a pouch of meat as his evening meal.

He also had some little treats while we

were out working. It was always more than sufficient to keep him happy and healthy. In fact, he normally left a quarter or so of his morning biscuits because it was too much for him.

A few days after he'd got his head caught in the tin can, however, I noticed that he was wolfing down all his breakfast in double-quick time. He was even licking the bowl clean.

He was also more demanding. I had always decided when to give him a reward for his tricks, but now he began to ask for snacks himself. There was something different about the way he pleaded for these snacks as well. It wasn't the usual plaintive, 'Puss in Boots' look.

I'm desperate for food! he seemed to say.

It was the same when we got home. He began to hassle me as soon as we

were in the door. Then he'd shovel everything down as fast as possible and give
me a look straight out of *Oliver Twist*.

Please, Dad. Can I have some more?

The alarming thing, however, was that
after a week or so of this behaviour, he
wasn't gaining any weight.

That's odd, I thought to myself.

Bob was also going to the toilet more
often. Over the years he'd overcome his
dislike of going in the litter tray at home
and did his business there in the mornings. He'd then go again when we were
out in London. Suddenly, however, this
habit changed. Now he was going three
times or more each day.

Bob started demanding to be taken to
the toilet more often at Angel. It was
always a real palaver, packing up and
heading over to the Green so that he

could get on with things, but it had to be done.

'What is wrong with you, Bob?' I said, losing patience with him after a few days of this.

He just gave me an aloof look. *Mind your own business*, he seemed to say.

Then one day I saw him deep in concentration, scooting his undercarriage on the carpet in the living room.

I wasn't best pleased.

'Bob, that's disgusting,' I scolded him. 'What do you think you're doing?'

But I soon realised that it must mean that he had a problem.

As usual, I was short of money and didn't really have enough to splash out on the expense of a vet. So the next morning on the way into work, I decided to drop into the local library and look up

Bob's symptoms on the internet. I guessed he had some kind of stomach parasite. It was consistent with going to the toilet more often and scooting his bottom on the floor.

During my childhood in Australia, I'd seen a couple of cats develop worms. It wasn't pleasant, and was also contagious. A lot of children in Australia used to contract worms from their cats. It was quite gross actually. I really hoped this wasn't the case with Bob.

Researching illness on the internet is always the biggest mistake you can make. Within half an hour, I'd convinced myself that Bob had a really serious kind of worm: a hookworm or a tapeworm. Neither is fatal, but both are really nasty, causing severe weight loss and a deterioration in the coat if untreated.

I knew the only thing I could do to be sure was to check his poo the next time he went to the toilet. I didn't have to wait long. Within about an hour of us settling down at Angel, he started making his tell-tale noises and gestures and I took him off to the Green. I braced myself to sneak a quick look before he covered up his business in the soft earth.

He didn't take kindly to my intrusion.

'Sorry, Bob, but I've got to take a peek,' I said, inspecting his droppings with a twig.

It may sound bizarre, but I was delighted when I saw some tiny, white wiggly creatures in there. It *was* worms, but only tiny little ones.

At least it's not tapeworm or hookworm, I consoled myself for the rest of that day.

I felt a slightly confusing mix of

emotions. The responsible cat owner in me was really miffed. I was so careful about Bob's diet, avoiding raw meats and other risky things. I also regularly checked for fleas, which can act as hosts for worms. Bob was also a really clean and healthy cat, and I made sure the flat was in a decent condition for him to live. I felt like it reflected badly on me.

'I've let you down, haven't I?' I told Bob. 'But at least I now know what to do. We need to visit the vet, mate.'

The Blue Cross is an animal charity that looks after sick and injured pets, and I knew the Blue Cross drop-in van was going to be at Islington Green the following day. So I made sure that I got a sample of Bob's morning poo in a plastic pill container, and we got there early to beat the queue.

The staff there knew us well. Bob had been microchipped here, and I'd spent the best part of a year dropping in to slowly pay off the fees for that and other treatments. I'd also had him checked out frequently for fleas and other parasites, ironically.

'Can you describe the problem?' asked the vet who was on duty that morning.

'He's eating all the time, and going to the toilet a lot,' I explained. 'He's also itching his bottom on the floor. So I checked his poo and found worms.'

The vet checked the sample I had brought. 'Yes, he's got worms I'm afraid, James,' he said. 'What's he been eating lately? Anything out of the ordinary? Been rummaging in the bins or anything like that?'

It was as if a light had gone on in my head. I felt so stupid.

'Yes!' I gasped. 'He got his head stuck in an old food can a little while ago. He must have found a piece of old chicken or other meat in there!'

How could I have failed to see that?

The vet gave me a course of medication and a plastic syringe I could use to put the medicine down Bob's throat.

'How long will it take to clear things up?' I asked.

'Should be on the mend within a few days, James,' he said. 'Let me know if the symptoms persist.'

Years earlier, I'd had to give Bob some antibiotics by hand, putting tablets in his mouth and then rubbing his throat to help them on their way down into his stomach. The syringe was supposed to make that process simpler. But Bob still had to trust me to put it down his throat.

Back at the flat that evening, I could tell that Bob didn't like the look of the syringe. But he trusted me enough to let me place it inside his mouth and release the tablet.

'You know I wouldn't do anything to you that wasn't absolutely necessary, don't you, Bob?' I told him, rubbing his throat.

He seemed to understand.

Bob was back to his normal self within a couple of days. He was soon eating and going to the toilet normally again.

As I thought about what had happened, I gave myself a ticking off. The responsibility of looking after Bob had been such a positive force in my life. But I needed to live up to that responsibility a little better. Bob wasn't a part-time job that I could clock into whenever the mood took me.

'I must never let a bin bag lie around like that again,' I said to myself.

Most of all, though, I breathed a sigh of relief. It wasn't often that Bob was off colour or ill, but whenever he was I always jumped to the worst conclusions. Over the past days I'd imagined Bob dying and having to carry on life without him. It was too scary to think about.

I always said that we were partners, that we needed each other equally. Deep down I believed that wasn't really true. I felt like I needed him more.

Chapter 10
Cat on a Hoxton Roof

Bob and I are a distinctive pair. There aren't many six-foot-tall blokes walking around the streets of London with a ginger cat sitting on their shoulders, after all.

For a few months during the summer and autumn of 2009, we made an even more eye-catching sight. Unfortunately, I was in too much pain to enjoy the attention.

The problems had begun the previous year, when I travelled to Australia to see my mother. My mum and I had always had a difficult relationship. Apart from a brief visit to London, the last time I'd seen her was when she'd seen me off at the airport aged 18 to 'make it' as a musician in London. In the lost decade that followed, we'd barely talked. Time had healed the wounds a little, so, when she offered to pay for me to visit her in Tasmania, I went.

With Bob's help, I'd just managed to make a massive breakthrough with my drug addiction. It had left me feeling weak, so I needed the break. Bob had stayed with my friend Belle, at her flat near Hoxton in north London, not too far from Angel.

There was always a risk of DVT

– deep vein thrombosis – when you were tall like me and sat without moving on a flight for hours. I had known about the risks, but despite doing my best to walk around the plane as often as possible, I'd come home with a nagging pain in my upper thigh.

At first it was manageable, and I dealt with it by taking ordinary painkillers. Slowly but surely, however, it grew worse. I began feeling as if my blood had stopped flowing and my muscles were seizing up. I felt as if I had the leg of a zombie.

The pain soon became so bad that I couldn't sit or lie down in a normal position. So whenever I was watching television or eating a meal at home in the flat, I had to sit with my leg on a cushion or another chair. At bedtime, I had to sleep the wrong way round with my foot raised up over the end of the bed head.

I went to see the doctor a couple of times, but they had only prescribed stronger painkillers. I'm sure they felt that my condition, whatever it was, was left over from my drug-abusing past. I didn't push it, but it reinforced that old feeling I'd had as a homeless person that I was invisible.

The real problem for me was that I still needed to earn a living. However uncomfortable I was, I still had to haul myself out of bed and head to Angel on a daily basis.

It wasn't easy. The moment I put my foot on the floor, pain shot up through my leg. I could only walk three or four steps at a time. So the walk to the bus stop became a marathon, often taking me twice or three times as long as it would normally.

Bob didn't know what to make of this at first. He kept giving me quizzical looks, as if to say, *What are you doing, mate?* But he soon worked out there was something wrong and started changing his behaviour.

In the morning, for instance, rather than greeting me with his usual pleading looks, he started looking at me with a slightly pitying expression.

Feeling any better today? he seemed to ask.

He began to walk alongside me rather than ride on my shoulders. He obviously preferred travelling on the upper deck, as I put it, but I think he could see I was in pain.

When he felt that I had been hobbling

along for too long, he would actually try to make me stop and sit down. He would cut across my path, steering me towards a bench or wall where I could take a break. I thought it was better to finish my journey rather than stopping every few steps so, for a while, it developed into a bit of a battle of wills.

Whenever he heard me complain about the pain, Bob would stop and give me a look.

Take a breather or sit down then, he seemed to say.

'No, Bob,' I would reply. 'I need to keep moving.'

If I hadn't been in so much agony, I'd probably have found it quite amusing to watch. We probably resembled a bickering old married couple.

To make life easier, I began staying

with Belle. Her flat was on the first floor rather than the fifth floor, which saved me a lot of aggravation. Getting to work from Belle's place was also less painful with a bus stop only yards away.

But the pain continued to grow worse.

'I need a crutch,' I decided one morning.

With Bob in tow, I'd headed into the pretty little park near Belle's flat and found a branch from a fallen tree that fitted perfectly under my arm. It allowed me to keep the weight off my painful leg when I walked.

I got a lot of very strange looks, understandably. With my long hair and shaggy beard, I must have looked like some kind of modern-day Merlin. The ginger cat sitting on my shoulders must have conjured up images of wizards walking around with their 'familiars'. The truth was that I didn't really care. Anything that eased the pain was a Godsend.

The Bobmobile was in the hallway back in Tottenham, gathering dust. There was no way I could cycle anywhere with the pain I was in.

Bob understood that there was something seriously wrong with me. Some mornings, as he watched me struggling to get my trousers on, he would give me a withering look.

Why are you doing this to yourself? he seemed to say. *Why don't you stay in bed?*

'I have no option, Bob,' I said through gritted teeth. 'We're skint, as usual.'

Standing at my pitch outside Angel tube station for five or six hours a day was becoming impossible.

Fortunately, one of the tube-station

florists saw the state I was in one day and came over to me, holding a couple of buckets that he used for his flowers.

'There you go, sit on that. And get Bob to sit on the other one,' he had said, giving me an encouraging pat on the back.

'Thanks,' I said gratefully. 'I really appreciate it.'

When I started sitting on the bucket, I was terrified that people simply wouldn't see me sitting there and I wouldn't sell any magazines. I should have known better. Bob took care of it.

During this period, he became a real little showman. He would rub up against me and give me a look, as if to say *Come on, mate, get the snacks out. Let's do some tricks and earn a few quid!*

I was certain he'd worked out that the

sooner we earned a decent amount of money, the sooner we could get home and rest my leg. It was eerie how he understood so much.

I wished I could see life so clearly sometimes.

Living at Belle's with Bob had its pros and cons. While I spent as much time as I could off my feet, Belle looked after me, cooking me nice meals and doing my laundry. Bob got on well with her too. During the time he'd spent with her while I was in Australia, they had clearly formed a strong bond. She was the only other person whom he would ever consider allowing to pick him up, for instance.

The previous year, when Bob had run

away from Angel one evening after being attacked by a dog, he'd headed for Belle's flat. It had taken me hours to work out that he'd taken refuge there. It had been the longest night of my life.

The closeness of their relationship certainly made life easier for me. But it also gave Bob licence to be mischievous.

One morning I got up and headed into the kitchen in my T-shirt and boxer shorts to make myself a cup of coffee, expecting to find Bob settled there. There was no sign of him. There was no sign of Belle either.

It had been raining heavily that morning but it was now bright and sunny and the temperature was rising. I noticed that Belle had already opened the window in the kitchen to let some fresh air into the flat.

'Bob, where are you, mate?' I said, searching the flat.

There was no sign of him in the sitting room or the hallway, so I headed to the back bedroom where Belle slept. When I saw the window there was ajar, I got an instant sinking feeling.

Belle's flat was on the first floor and the back bedroom window overlooked the roof of the extension on the ground floor flat below us. That roof overlooked a yard and the car park for the building. From there it was a short walk to the main road, one of the busiest in that part of London.

'Oh, no, Bob,' I gasped, squeezing my head out of the window. 'You haven't gone out there, have you?'

Sure enough, five flats along from Belle's, there was Bob, sunning himself on the roof.

'Bob!' I yelled in alarm. I was concerned that he might slide off the slippery roof, or go down into the yard and out through the car park on to the main road.

He slowly turned his head in my direction.

What's wrong? he seemed to say.

Chapter 11
Asking Questions

I panicked and took the security screws off the window, so that I could open it fully and climb out on to the roof. I still hadn't managed to put on any clothes.

The slate tiles were slippery from the rain earlier in the morning, so keeping a grip wasn't easy. I was in agony with my leg. Somehow, however, I managed to cross the rooftops to where Bob was sitting.

I was on a wasted mission.

Bob instantly picked himself up and scuttled back across the rooftops. When I tried to grab at him, he just growled at me and made a sudden spurt towards Belle's open window, disappearing back indoors.

It took me a few minutes to scramble back across the slippery slates. To my complete embarrassment, a couple of faces appeared in the windows. The looks on their faces spoke volumes. They were a mix of shock, mild pity and hilarity.

Moments after I got back into the safety of the flat, I heard the front door closing. Belle was standing in the hallway with a small bag of groceries.

She burst out laughing.

'Where have you been?' she giggled.

'On the roof trying to rescue Bob,' I said.

'Oh, he goes out there all the time,' she said. 'He even goes down into the yard sometimes. He always comes back up.'

'I really wish you'd told me that sooner,' I complained, shuffling off to finally put on some clothes.

Soon after that, it was Belle who was suffering from Bob's playful ways.

As I'd discovered the hard way, Bob loved exploring the back of Belle's block of flats. He took full advantage of the fact that he was on the first rather than the fifth floor.

I knew that it was part of Bob's DNA to hunt. Cats are seriously effective predators. One day we were sitting in the front room when he arrived with a small mouse dangling from his mouth. He'd placed it carefully at my feet, as if he was offering me a gift.

'Bob, you will make yourself sick again if you eat that,' I scolded.

He soon became bolder.

One morning, I was lying on my bed reading when I heard the most almighty scream.

Aaargh!

I jumped up and ran into the living room where Belle was doing some iron-ing. There, sitting on top of a pile of freshly pressed shirts and bed sheets, was a little brown frog.

'James, James, pick it up, get rid of it. Please,' she shrieked.

Bob was in the doorway with a

mischievous expression on his face. It was as if he knew exactly what had happened.

I got hold of the little frog and cupped it in my hands. I then walked round the area at the back of the building to release it, with Bob following me every step of the way.

About an hour or so later, I heard another scream, accompanied by the sound of something hitting a wall.

'What is it now?' I said, heading into the hall.

Belle was standing at one end of the corridor with her hands on her head and a horrified expression on her face. She pointed down the corridor at a pair of slippers that she'd clearly thrown down the hallway.

'It's inside my slipper now,' she said.

'What's inside your slipper?' I said, puzzled.

'The frog.'

I had to suppress a laugh. But, again, I retrieved the frog and took it out to the garden. Again Bob marched behind me, trying to look like it was a pure coincidence that this frog had now appeared inside the flat twice.

'Stay there, mate,' I said. I had to make sure I disposed of the frog properly this time.

Bob looked at me disapprovingly, then turned and slinked off back into the house as if to say, *you're really no fun at all!*

As comfortable as we were at Belle's, after a while I began to realise that it wasn't ideal, in particular for my relationship with Bob.

The pain in my leg had made me short-tempered and generally less fun to be around than usual. Sensing that I wasn't in the best of moods when I woke up, Bob wouldn't always come into the bedroom for an early morning play. Often Belle would rustle up a breakfast for him instead. He would also head off out of the window to hunt and would sometimes be gone for long stretches. I imagined he was having a great time out there.

I also had a very strong suspicion that he was eating elsewhere too. When Belle or I put down a bowl for him, he did little more than play with his food.

At first my heart sank a little. *He's eating in the bins again*, I said to myself.

One day, when we were heading out to work, I saw an elderly gentleman downstairs, collecting his mail. Bob saw him and fixed him with a knowing stare.

'Hello, young fellow,' the man said. 'Nice to see you again.'

Suddenly I remembered that children's book *Six Dinner Sid* by Inga Moore, about a cat that charms its way into the affections of everyone on his street, earning himself a dinner in every house each night. Bob had pulled the same stunt. He had become Six Dinner Bob.

It was a sign that Bob was getting used to life without me at the centre of his world. Lying there at night, trying to think about anything and everything but the throbbing pain in my leg, I began to ask myself something I'd not asked in all the time Bob and I been together. Would he be better off without me?

Who needed to be out on the streets in all kinds of weather, being poked and prodded by passers-by? Especially when there were friendlier, less complicated souls around to give you a square meal every day.

I'd always felt that I could give Bob as good a life as anyone else. Now, for the first time since we'd got together, I wasn't so sure.

Chapter 12
Bob's Choice

Another time, I was limping through the car park in a local supermarket when I saw a wheelchair, sitting there unoccupied. The thought of being able to travel around without having to put any weight on my foot was really tempting. For a split second, I thought about stealing it. I was ashamed of myself the moment the idea entered my head.

I also found myself thinking more and more about Bob. Or more specifically, losing Bob. The worse my leg became, the more I became convinced that he was ready to leave. I imagined him in the company of the old man next door, being pampered and fussed over. I pictured him lying on the sunny roof at Belle's while I hobbled off to sell *The Big Issue* on my own.

Because of the pain, I had less patience for Bob than usual and wouldn't play with him. Sometimes he would try to drape himself around my leg, which I found unbearable. By now my leg was a violent, red colour and the pain was relentless.

'Go away and play somewhere else, Bob,' I'd say, brushing him to one side.

He'd reluctantly head out of the

bedroom door, throwing me a disappointed look as he went.

It's hardly a surprise that he's starting to look elsewhere for affection, I thought. *I'm not much of a friend to him at the moment.*

At last, one morning I woke up and decided that enough was enough. I didn't care what the doctors thought about me and my past: I wanted some answers. I wanted this problem to go away. I got dressed, grabbed my crutch and headed for the local surgery.

'That's an interesting crutch you have there, Mr Bowen,' the doctor said when I turned up in the consulting room.

'Necessity is the mother of invention,' I said.

He began casting an eye over my thigh and leg.

'This doesn't look too good,' he said.

'You need to keep pressure off that leg for a week or so and you need a blood test to check for clotting in the blood cells.' He looked at my crutch. 'And I think we can do better than a tree branch.'

By the end of the morning I was the proud owner of a pair of proper metallic crutches, complete with rubber grips, arm holders and shock absorbers. I didn't waste any time and went to have the blood test done the following day.

A couple of days later, I rang the clinic.

'Any news on my blood test?' I asked.

The female doctor confirmed my worst suspicions.

'You have a deep vein thrombosis, or DVT. It means you have a blood clot in your leg. So I need you to go to University College Hospital for tests,' she told me.

In a way it was a relief. I'd always suspected the long flight to and from Australia had caused the problem. But it was worrying too. I knew that DVT could cause heart attacks and strokes in particular.

When I got to the hospital I was told that, sure enough, I had a large blood clot in my leg.

'The hot weather probably set it off and then you made it worse by walking around on it,' said the doctor. 'I'll give you some medicine that should sort it out.'

I was relieved. But I didn't pay any attention to the leaflet that came with the medicine that explained about certain side effects.

A few nights after I started taking the tablets, I woke up to find my leg was covered in blood. The sheets of my bed were soaked red as well.

Bob had been fast asleep in the corner, but woke up. He could tell there was something wrong and shot up to stand at my side.

'I have to get to a hospital,' I told him, 'and fast.'

I threw on a pair of jeans and a jumper and ran out of the flat, heading towards Tottenham High Road where I figured I had a chance of catching a bus.

When I got to the hospital, they admitted me immediately. I was kept in for two days while they sorted out my medication.

'We'll try another drug,' said a doctor. 'It shouldn't have the same effect.'

But it didn't work. Even after a couple of weeks, my leg was no better. I couldn't walk more than two paces, even with the crutches. I was now beginning to despair. Once again, I began to imagine losing my leg altogether.

I went back to the hospital.

'Help me,' I begged.

This time they decided to keep me in for a week to check me out more thoroughly.

'Come back tomorrow,' they said. 'We'll have a bed for you then.'

I wasn't best pleased about it. But I knew that I simply couldn't carry on in this condition. I went home that night and explained the situation to Belle.

'I'll look after Bob,' Belle assured me.

This was a huge comfort. I knew Bob was happy in Belle's flat. The following morning I got up and packed a small bag of stuff to take to hospital.

I'm not the greatest hospital patient. I lay there worrying about everything – my leg, my long-term health, my pitch at Angel and, as always, the lack of money. I also lay there and fretted about Bob.

I could see that I'd not been the most brilliant company in recent weeks. Maybe it was time for us to go our separate ways. Should I ask Belle if she wanted to keep him? Or the nice bloke next door? I would be devastated to lose him. He was my best friend, my rock. I needed him to keep me on the straight and narrow, to keep me sane. But at the same time, I had to make the right choice for Bob. I really didn't know what to do.

Then it struck me. It wasn't my decision.

They say cats choose you, not the other way round. For whatever reason,

Bob had seen something in me that made him want to stick around. Now I had to wait to see if he'd choose me again. If he wanted to remain with me, then it would be his decision. And his alone.

I'd find out his answer soon enough, I felt sure.

Chapter 13
The Final Step

The doctors in the hospital increased the dose of my medicine and they also decided to keep me in a little longer.

'Just for a couple more days,' the doctor told me. 'We want to make sure it works this time.'

The new dosage finally sorted out my DVT. When I looked at my leg the swelling was beginning to go down and the colour returning to normal. The nurses and doctors could see this as well.

'It's not good for you lying there all day, Mr Bowen,' one of the nurses kept saying to me. 'Try walking up and down the corridor at least a couple of times a day.'

It was a joy to be able to walk around without wincing so much. It still hurt, but it wasn't anywhere near as bad as before.

'I think it's time to go home,' smiled one of the doctors.

I texted Belle with the good news.

'Great!' she texted back. 'I'll meet you at the hospital later.'

By the time I'd filled in the paperwork, got dressed and gathered together my belongings, it was nearly evening.

'Meet me outside by the art sculpture,'

Belle texted. 'Can't come into hospital. Will explain when I see you.'

I limped my way to the exit on Euston Road. I'd heard people at the hospital talking about the art sculpture outside: a giant, six-ton polished pebble. I leaned on it for a moment or two as I tried to catch my breath, after walking what seemed like miles along the corridors without the aid of crutches.

I soon saw Belle emerging from the bus stop across the road. She was carrying a large, holdall style bag which, I assumed, had some clean clothes and my jacket in it.

As she got closer, I saw a flash of ginger fur poking out of the unzipped top of the bag. Then, as she reached the bottom of the hospital steps, I saw a little head poking out.

'Bob,' I said, excited.

The moment he heard my voice, Bob began scrambling out of the bag. We were still a few feet apart when he launched himself off the bag towards me. It was the most athletic leap I'd ever seen him make, and that was saying a lot.

'Whoaah there, fella,' I said, lurching forward to catch him and holding him close to my chest.

He pinned himself to me like a limpet clinging on to a rock that was being pounded by waves. He then nuzzled his head in my neck and started rubbing me with his cheeks.

'Hope you don't mind, but that's why I couldn't come in. I had to bring him,' Belle said, beaming. 'He saw me packing a few things for you and started going crazy. I think he knew I was coming to get you.'

Whatever doubts I'd had about our future together were swept away in that instant. On the way home, Bob was all over me – literally. He sat on my lap, crawled on my shoulders and sat up with his paws on my chest, purring away contentedly.

It was as if he never wanted to let me go again. I felt exactly the same way.

'I thought Bob wanted to leave me,' I told Belle.

'Far from it,' she laughed. 'The whole time you were in the flat, he was desperate to help you. Didn't you realise?'

Belle told me that whenever I had been asleep in my room, Bob would check up on me.

'He'd give you a little tap on the

forehead and wait for you to react. I think he just wanted to make sure you were still with us,' she smiled.

At other times, she told me, he would wrap himself around my leg.

'It was like he wanted to take away the pain,' she said. 'He was definitely trying to do something about it.'

I hadn't realised any of this. Instead, whenever Bob had tried to help or comfort me, I'd driven him away. I'd been selfish. Bob loved – and needed – me as much as I loved and needed him. I wouldn't forget that.

A few weeks after getting back on my feet, I took the most important step I'd made in years. Perhaps in my entire life.

I'd been attending a drug clinic for several years now. I'd arrived there a mess, addicted and on a fast track to an early grave. Thanks to a brilliant collection of counsellors and nurses, I'd been hauling myself back from the brink ever since. I had started taking a prescription drug that I needed before I could come off drugs altogether. It had been a pretty seamless process, much easier than I'd anticipated.

'A few more days of taking it,' explained my drug counsellor, 'and I think you'll be ready to call yourself clean.'

I should have been delighted. It was time for that soft aeroplane landing that one of my counsellors had talked about. But I was curiously on edge, and remained that way for the next two days. It was almost as if I was waiting for something awful to happen.

Bob sensed that I needed a little more TLC. He wasn't obvious about it. He didn't need to perform any of his late night diagnoses or tap me on the head to check I was still breathing. He just sat a few inches closer on the sofa and gave me an extra rub of his head on my neck every now and again.

Five or six days after I had been given my final prescription, I pulled the foil container out of its packet and saw that there was just one tablet left.

I squeezed the oval-shaped pill out, placed it under my tongue until it had all dissolved, and then downed a glass of water. I scrunched the foil up into a ball and threw it on the floor for Bob to chase.

'There you go, mate,' I said. 'That's the last one of those you'll get to play with.'

That night, I felt sure that my body was going to be racked by withdrawal pangs. I expected nightmares, visions, restless twisting and turning. But there was nothing. The moment my head hit the pillow, I was out like a light.

When I woke up the next morning, I gathered my senses and thought to myself: *That's it. I'm clean.*

I looked out of the window at the London skyline. It wasn't a glorious blue sky, unfortunately. But it certainly was a clear one. And it seemed somehow brighter.

I knew that the days, weeks, months and years stretching ahead of me weren't going to be easy. There would be times when I knew that niggling temptation would return, and I'd think about taking something to deaden the pain, to kill the senses.

Loneliness and hopelessness had driven me to drugs in the first place. But I was determined that wasn't going to happen again. Life wasn't perfect, far from it. But it was a million times better than it had been when I'd formed my addiction. I could see a way forward. I knew that I could soldier on.

From that day onwards, each time I felt myself weakening I told myself: *Hold on. I'm not sleeping rough, I'm not alone, it's not hopeless. I don't need drugs any more.*

A month or so after I'd taken that last tablet, my drug counsellor signed me off.

'I don't need to see you again,' he said as he ushered me out of the door. 'Stay in touch, but good luck. And well done.'

And I am happy to say I have not had to see him since.

Chapter 14
Big Night Out

As we walked south across the Thames at Waterloo Bridge, the lights of the Houses of Parliament and the London Eye blazed bright in the late November night sky and the pavement was busy with people. It was approaching 10.30pm, the end of their day. For me and Bob, on the other hand, it was the beginning of what promised to be a very, very long night.

The Big Issue was staging an event called 'The Big Night Out' to coincide with the eighteenth birthday of the magazine. They were organising an eighteen-mile walk through the streets of London in the middle of the night to mark the occasion.

The idea was that ordinary people could walk through the deserted city between 10.30 pm and 7am with a group of *The Big Issue* vendors, so that they could learn a little about the reality of living rough and sleeping on the streets.

I'd made the decision to take part for a couple of reasons. Firstly, it was a chance to earn a few extra pounds. Every vendor that took part in the walk was eligible for 25 to 30 free copies of *The Big Issue*. That meant that I could earn about £60 if I sold them all.

Secondly, it was an opportunity to talk to people about the magazine and the lives of the people who sold it. *The Big Issue* was, without question, the salvation for many people who lived on the streets. It had certainly helped give me direction and purpose – not to mention enough money to keep the wolf from the door. It was important to share that with people.

We were meeting at the IMAX cinema on the south side of Waterloo Bridge. It was a fitting location. Not so long ago, the area had been home to the shanty town that Londoners knew as Cardboard City. During the 1980s and early 1990s, it had become a home for more than 200 'rough sleepers'. Many people created homes for themselves just from wooden pallets and cardboard boxes. Some even had living rooms and bedrooms with mattresses. I'd stayed there briefly during its final days, at the end of 1997 and early 1998, when everyone was evicted to make way for the IMAX cinema.

My memories of the place were sketchy, but when I walked into the IMAX I saw the organisers of the walk had created a little picture exhibition on the history of Cardboard City. With Bob on my shoulders, I scanned the grainy black and white images for faces that I recognised. As it turned out, I was looking in the wrong place.

'Hello, James,' a female voice said behind me. I recognised it straight away.

'Hello, Billie,' I said.

Back around the year 2000, when my life was at its lowest ebb, Billie and I had become friendly, helping each other out and keeping each other company. We had huddled up against the cold together at the cold-weather shelters that charities like Centrepoint and St Mungo's used to put up during the winter months.

'How's it going, Billie?' I said.

'Good,' she told me. 'I've turned my life around.'

Billie told me how she had been sleeping rough in central London ten years earlier when she was disturbed from her sleep by a seller of *The Big Issue*.

'At first I was annoyed at being woken up by him,' she said. 'I hadn't even known what the magazine was. But then I looked at it and grasped the idea.'

Billie had managed to rebuild her life. Now she was a 'poster child' for The Big Issue Foundation.

We reminisced about the bad old days over a cup of tea. It was hard to remember that time because it was all a blur. But we were still here. Goodness knows how many of the people who had been on the streets with us hadn't been so lucky.

Billie was very committed to this walk. 'It will give people an idea what we had to go through,' she said. 'They won't be able to slip off home into a warm bed. They'll have to stay out there with us.'

Billie had a dog, a lively Border collie called Solo. Solo and Bob weighed each other up for a few minutes but then decided there was nothing to worry about.

Just before 10.30pm John Bird, the founder of *The Big Issue,* arrived. He fired everyone up with an inspiring speech about the difference the magazine had made during its eighteen years. By now a hundred or more people had gathered, along with a couple of dozen vendors, co-ordinators and staff. We all filed out into the night, ready for John Bird to do the countdown.

'Three, two, one,' he shouted and then we were off.

'Here we go, Bob,' I said, making sure he was positioned comfortably on my shoulders.

On the one hand, I was really worried about whether my leg would stand up to eighteen miles of wear and tear, but, on the other, I was just delighted to be off my crutches and walking normally again. So, as we set off on the first leg around the South Bank and across the Millennium Bridge, I told myself to simply enjoy it.

As usual, Bob was soon attracting a lot of attention. There was a real party atmosphere, and a lot of the charity fundraisers began taking snaps of him as we walked. He wasn't in the friendliest of moods, which was understandable. It was way past his bedtime and he could feel the cold coming off the Thames. But I had a generous supply of snacks as well as some water and a bowl for him. I'd also been assured there would be a bowl of milk for him at the stop-off points.

We will give it our best shot, I said to myself.

Chapter 15
Calling It Quits

Bob and I settled into a group in the middle of the procession as it worked its way along the riverside. They were a mix of students and charity workers, as well as a couple of middle-aged women. One of the ladies started asking me questions.

'Where do you come from?' she asked. 'How did you end up on the streets?'

'I came to London from Australia when I was eighteen,' I explained. 'I was born in the UK, but my parents separated and my mum took me with her when she moved down under. We moved around a lot and I became a bit of a troublemaker. When I came to London, I hoped to make it as a musician but it didn't really work out. That's when my troubles started and I ended up on the streets, and that's where *The Big Issue* came in.'

After about an hour and a half, we made it to the first stopping-off point – the Hispaniola floating restaurant on the Embankment on the north side of the Thames.

I helped myself to some of the soup on offer, while Bob lapped up some milk that someone had kindly sorted out for him. I was feeling pretty positive about the walk now and was already totting up the miles that I'd done – and how many more were to come.

But then, as we were heading off the ship, we had a bit of a setback. Perhaps because he knew that my leg still wasn't a hundred per cent, Bob decided to walk off the boat instead of riding on my shoulders. As he padded his way down the ramp, he walked straight into another vendor who was coming up the walkway with a dog, a Staffie.

The Staffie instantly went for Bob.

'Whoa!' I said, and jumped in front of it with my arms and legs out to stop him lunging at Bob.

Staffies do get a bad reputation for being violent, but I don't think this one was. He was just being curious, not evil. Unfortunately, however, it freaked Bob out a bit. As we started our walk again, he wrapped himself tightly around me. I think this was partly because he was nervous but also to protect himself against the cold. There was a bone-chilling mist rising off the Thames.

'I think we might go home,' I told a couple of the organisers. I was worried about Bob now, especially as the weather looked to be getting worse.

'Stay a bit longer,' they persuaded me. So we did.

As we headed away from the river, the temperatures lifted a little bit. We wound our way through the West End and headed north. I got talking to a pretty young blonde girl and her French boyfriend.

'How did you and your cat get together?' they wanted to know.

Talking about Bob suited me fine and we had a really nice chat together for the next part of the walk. But as the night wore on, I began to feel a throbbing pain in my thigh, where the DVT had been. It was inevitable. But it was still annoying.

For the next hour or so I ignored it. But whenever we stopped for a cup of tea I could feel an acute shooting pain. Bob and I had been falling further and further behind, eventually reaching the back of the line. And after taking a couple of breaks to let Bob do his business, suddenly I realised that we had cut loose from the rest.

The next official stop was a few miles away. I really didn't think I could make it that far. So when we passed a bus stop with a night bus that headed in our direction, I made a decision.

'What do you think, Bob, shall we call it quits?'

Bob didn't say anything, but I could tell that he was ready for his bed. When a bus loomed into view and opened its doors, he bounded on board and on to a seat, bristling with pleasure at being in the warm.

The bus was surprisingly busy given how late it was. Bob and I were surrounded by a cluster of clubbers, happy from their night out in the West End or wherever it was they'd been. There were also a couple of lonely-looking guys, sitting there as if they were on the road to nowhere. I'd been there and done that, of course. I not only had the T-shirt, I had a wardrobe full of them.

But that was the past. Tonight it felt very different. Tonight I felt rather pleased with myself. Walking a dozen or so miles might not have seemed much of an achievement to some people but, for me, it was the equivalent of running the London Marathon.

I'd also been reunited with some familiar faces. It had been a joy to see Billie again and to see how well she was doing. All in all, I felt like I'd done something positive, that I'd given something back. I'd spent so many years taking from people, because I thought I had nothing to give. Tonight had shown me that wasn't true. Everyone has something to contribute, no matter how small. Maybe tonight, I'd opened a few people's eyes to the reality of life on the streets. That wasn't to be dismissed. It was worth something.

And so, I began to quietly tell myself, was I.

Chapter 16
A Tale of Two Cities

I drew back my bedroom curtains and looked out across the north London rooftops. Thick banks of iron-grey clouds were stacked up overhead and I could hear the wind gusting and whistling outside. If ever there was a day to stay at home and wrap up warm, today was that day. Unfortunately, that wasn't a luxury I could afford.

Things were tight at the moment. Both the gas and electric meters needed topping up, so the flat was icy cold. Bob had started snuggling up close to my bed at night, hoping to soak up some of the heat from my duvet. The bottom line was that I had to keep selling *The Big Issue*, and I couldn't afford to take the day off.

The only question was whether Bob was going to come with me. As always, it would be his decision. It was a decision he generally got right.

Cats – like a lot of other animals – are very good at 'reading' the weather and other natural events. They are very skilled at predicting earthquakes and tsunamis, for instance. Bob certainly sensed when rain was in the air. He hated getting wet and often refused to come out when the weather seemed fine, only for the heavens to open an hour or two later when I'd taken to the streets on my own.

So when I showed him his lead and scarf and he came towards me as normal, I guessed that his weather forecasting instincts were telling him it was safe to venture out.

'You sure about this, Bob?' I said. 'I'm happy to go on my own today.'

I picked out one of his thickest and warmest scarves. Then I wrapped it snugly around his neck and we headed out into the greyness.

The moment I set foot on the street outside, the wind cut through me like a scalpel. I felt Bob's tummy curling itself even tighter than usual around my neck.

Fortunately our regular bus service

appeared within a few minutes, and Bob and I were soon on board. Feeling warmth on the back of my leg from a heater lifted my spirits briefly. But things soon took a turn for the worse.

We'd barely been on the road for ten minutes when I noticed the first flakes of snow swirling around outside. Within moments, the air was thick with chunky, white flakes that were already sticking to the pavement and the roofs of parked cars.

'This doesn't look good,' I said to Bob, who was absorbed by the transformation that was taking place on the streets outside.

A mile or so from Angel, the traffic had ground to an almost total standstill. I faced a real dilemma. It was going to be tough to earn a few quid today, and conditions were going to be really challenging. But at the same time, I was short of money. I wasn't sure I had enough to get back home, let alone put a few quid in the electricity meter over the next day or so.

'Come on, Bob, if we're going to earn anything today we'd better walk the last mile,' I said, reluctantly.

We hopped out on to the pavement. For Bob, this was a fascinating new world to explore. I had put him on my shoulders as usual, but I'd barely walked a few yards before he was repositioning himself ready to clamber down to earth.

As I put him down, I realised that it was the first time Bob had been out and about in snow. I watched him dabbing a paw into the powdery whiteness, then standing back to admire the print he'd left behind. For a moment I imagined what it must be like to see the world through his eyes. It must have seemed so bizarre, to see everything suddenly turned white.

'Come on, mate, we can't hang around all day,' I said after a minute or two.

Bob was still having a great time lifting his feet in and out of the ever-deepening snow. Eventually, however, it got so deep that his belly was lined with white crystals.

'Let's get you back up here,' I said, grabbing him and sticking back on my shoulders.

The problem now was that the snow was falling so steadily and heavily that it was settling on both of us. Every few yards I had to brush an inch of fresh snow off my shoulders, then do the same thing to Bob.

I had a broken old umbrella but it was next to useless in the strong winds. I gave up on it within minutes.

'This is no good, Bob. I think we need to find you a coat,' I said.

I dived into a small convenience store, stamping my feet clean of snow in the doorway.

At first the owner, an Indian lady, looked shocked to see the pair of us standing there. This was hardly surprising. We must have made a bizarre sight. But her mood soon thawed.

'You are brave walking about in this weather,' she smiled.

'I don't know about brave,' I said. 'Mad might be closer to the truth.'

I wasn't quite sure what I was looking for. At first I wondered about buying a new umbrella, but they were too expensive. I only had a small amount of change. But then I had an idea and headed for the area where the kitchen supplies were stocked. I saw a roll of small, heavy-duty bin liners.

'That might do the trick, Bob,' I said. 'How much for a single bag?' I asked the lady.

'I can't sell them as singles. I have to sell you the whole roll. It's £2,' she said.

I didn't want to fork out that much. I really was broke. But then I noticed she had little black carrier bags on the counter top for customers to carry their shopping.

'Is there any chance I could take one of those?' I said.

'OK,' she said. 'They are 5p.'

'I'll take one,' I said. 'Do you have any scissors?'

'Scissors?'

'Yes, I want to make a hole in it.'

This time she looked at me as if I truly was off my rocker. But she dipped down behind the counter and produced a small pair of sewing scissors.

'Perfect,' I said.

I grabbed the closed end of the bag and cut a small semicircle about the size of Bob's head. I then opened the bag up and slipped Bob's head through it. The improvised poncho fitted like a glove and covered his body and legs perfectly.

'Oh, I see,' the lady said, laughing. 'Very clever. That should do the trick.'

It took us about fifteen minutes to get to Angel. One or two people shot us funny looks as we walked along, but most were more concerned with getting themselves from A to B safely in the drifting snow.

I knew there was no way we were going to be able to survive outside the tube at our normal selling pitch. The pavement was thick with slushy snow. So Bob and I positioned ourselves in the nearest underpass where the bulk of commuters were taking refuge.

I didn't want to keep Bob out in the cold for too long, so I put some extra effort into selling the magazines I had. Fortunately, a lot of people seemed to take pity on us and dipped into their pockets. My pile of magazines was soon dwindling.

By late afternoon, I'd made enough cash to keep us going for a day or two.

'Now, all we've got to do is get home,' I said to Bob as we once more bent ourselves into the icy winds and headed back to the bus stop.

Working on the streets of London really was a tale of two cities, as I was reminded again a few days later.

I was standing just outside Angel tube station around lunchtime, with Bob on my shoulders, when I noticed a bit of a commotion going on inside at the ticket gate where passengers emerged from the trains below. A group of people were having an animated conversation with the attendants. When it was over, they started heading in our direction.

I recognised the large, slightly scruffy, blond-haired figure at the centre of the group immediately. It was the Mayor of

London, Boris Johnson. He was with a young boy, his son I assumed, and a small group of smartly dressed assistants. They were marching straight towards my exit.

'How about a *Big Issue*, Boris?' I said, waving a magazine in the air.

'I'm in a bit of a rush,' he said, looking flustered. 'Hold on.'

To his credit, he started digging around in his pockets and produced a pile of coins, which he dropped into my hands.

'There you go,' he said. 'More valuable than British pounds.'

I didn't understand what he meant, but was grateful nevertheless.

'Thanks very much indeed for supporting Bob and me,' I said, handing him a magazine.

As he took it, he smiled and tilted his head slightly at Bob.

'That's a nice cat you've got there,' he said.

'Oh yes, he's a star,' I said. 'He's even got his own travelcard.'

'Amazing,' he said, before heading off.

'Good luck, Boris,' I said as he disappeared from view.

Chapter 17

Trouble on the Street

I hadn't wanted to be rude and check what Boris Johnson had given me a moment or two earlier, but, judging by the weight and number of the coins, it felt way more than the cover price of the magazine.

'That was generous of him, wasn't it, Bob?' I said, fishing around for the coins, which I'd hurriedly stuffed in my jacket pocket.

As I looked at the small pile of cash, however, my heart sank.

'Oh no, Bob,' I said. 'He gave me Swiss francs! That's what he meant when he said *more valuable than British pounds.*'

Except, of course, they weren't more valuable.

While foreign bank notes can be exchanged at most banks and *bureaux de change*, coins cannot. They were worthless. To me, at least.

It wasn't the first time something like this had happened to me.

A few years earlier, I'd been busking in Covent Garden when a very grand-looking character with a mane of grey hair reached into his trouser pocket and pulled out a scrunched-up note. It was red and looked like a big denomination, possibly

171

a £50 note. That was the only note I knew that had red in it.

'There you go, my man,' he said, thrusting it into my hand.

'Thanks very much indeed,' I said.

I waited a few minutes until he had gone before studying the scrunched-up note more closely.

It wasn't a £50 note. As I'd thought, it was red, but it had a picture of a bearded bloke I'd never seen before on it. It also had the number 100 written on it and was covered in some kind of Eastern European language. The only word that looked familiar was *Srbije*. I had no idea what it was or what it might be worth. So I packed up my stuff and headed for a shop that I knew changed foreign money and was open late for tourists.

'Can you tell me what this is worth,

please?' I said to the girl who was behind the window.

She was puzzled. 'I don't recognise it,' she said. 'Let me check with someone else.'

She went into a back office where I could see an older bloke sitting. After a short conversation she came back.

'It's one hundred Serbian dinar,' she said.

That sounded hopeful.

'It's worth just over 70p,' she said. 'So we can't exchange it.'

I felt disappointed. I'd secretly hoped that it might be enough money to get me and Bob through the weekend. Fat chance.

I was fed up with living off my wits on the streets. And I was fed up with being humiliated by those who had absolutely no idea of the life I was having to lead. There were times when I was close to breaking point. A few days after that incident with the Mayor, I felt like I had reached it.

Bob and I finished work early and took the tube to Victoria Station. As we weaved our way through the tunnels, Bob walked ahead of me on his lead. He knew we were going to meet my father.

Meeting my dad was something I'd begun to do more regularly in recent months. Spending a lot of my childhood in Australia meant I didn't see him much, but we'd become closer when I'd started cleaning up my act, and had got into the habit of meeting for a few drinks and a meal at a pub at Victoria Station. The staff there were pretty friendly and would let me slip Bob in provided I kept him hidden from the other punters. I'd learned to keep him under a table where he was happy snoozing. It was always my dad's treat. Well, I was never going to have the money to treat him, was I?

As usual, he was waiting there for me.

'So what's your news?'

'Not a lot,' I said. 'I'm getting cheesed off with selling *The Big Issue*. It's too dangerous. And London is full of people who don't care about you.'

'You need to get yourself a proper job, Jamie,' he said. (He was the only person who called me that.)

'That's easier said than done, Dad,' I said.

My dad was a hard worker who had

always been his own boss. I don't think he understood why I hadn't been able to do the same thing. To his credit, he'd tried to help but it hadn't panned out. He had remarried since splitting with my mum, and had two children, my half-siblings Caroline and Anthony, to look after. It got complicated.

'What about training in computing or something like that? There are loads of courses around,' he said.

This was true, but I didn't have the qualifications to get on most courses.

My dad said he'd ask around to see if there was anything going. 'But things are pretty rough everywhere at the moment,' he said, holding up a copy of the evening paper. 'Every time I look at the paper it's all doom and gloom. People losing their jobs everywhere.'

I knew he was frustrated by the way I lived my life. Deep down I knew he felt I wasn't trying. I understood why he felt that way, but the truth was that I was trying. Just in my own way.

To lighten things up a little we talked a bit about his family and my half-brother and -sister.

'What are you doing for Christmas?' he asked at one point.

'I'm just going to spend it with Bob,' I said. 'We enjoy being together.'

My dad didn't really get my relationship with Bob. Tonight, as usual, he stroked him occasionally and kept an eye on him when I popped to the toilet. He even got the waitress to bring him a saucer of milk and gave him a couple of snacks. But he wasn't a natural cat lover. And on the one or two occasions when I had talked about how much Bob helped me in sorting myself out, he just looked baffled. I suppose I couldn't blame him for that.

We spent an hour and a half together, but then he had to catch a train back to south London. He gave me a few quid to tide me over and we agreed to see each other again in a few weeks' time.

'Look after yourself, Jamie,' he said.

The station was still busy. I had a few magazines left in my satchel so decided to try and shift them before heading home. I found an empty pitch outside the railway station and was soon doing pretty well.

Bob had a full stomach and was on good form. People were stopping and making a fuss. I was just weighing up whether to stay or head home when trouble reared its head again.

I knew the men were going to be a problem the moment I set eyes on them heading across the road towards the main entrance to Victoria Station. I recognised one of them from my days selling *The Big Issue* in Covent Garden. His mate wasn't familiar, but I could tell he was a rough character. He was a big brute and was built like a sack of potatoes.

I was worried that they were heading in our direction. Sure enough, they were soon outside the tube station entrance. The bigger of the two men made a bee-line for me. He was every bit as aggressive as he looked.

'Oi, you, get lost,' he said, sticking his big red face close to mine. His breath stank.

Bob, as always, had spotted the danger and was hissing at him already. I wasn't going to be intimidated and stuck my ground.

'I've got a right to sell here and I've just got these few magazines to sell,' I said. 'You know you don't have any magazines and all you're looking to do is intimidate people – what you are doing is wrong. I've seen you beg before. You are nothing but a leech. I know you're forcing your mate to beg for you too.'

'You've got two minutes to pack your stuff up and leave,' he said. He then pushed his way into the crowds.

People were flooding in and out of the station, so I lost him and his mate for a few minutes. I was hoping that they were going to disappear. No such luck.

In hardly any time, the big guy reappeared, looking even angrier than before.

'Didn't you hear what I told you?' he snarled.

The next thing I knew he had hit me. He just walked up to me and punched me on the nose. It happened so fast, I didn't even see him pull back his arm. He just jabbed a giant fist into my face. I didn't have a hope of deflecting the blow.

Blood came gushing out of my nose. Bob meowed in concern.

I decided this wasn't a fight I could win. There was no sign of the police, so I was on my own against a pretty nasty pair of individuals. Working on the streets was risky, I knew that. But at times like this, it was downright dangerous.

'Come on, Bob, let's get out of here,' I said.

I felt a mix of anger and despair. I

couldn't take much more of this life. But I couldn't see how on earth I was going to break free. Suddenly, all that talk with my father of jobs and training seemed ridiculous. Who was going to give me a job and pay me a decent salary? On that day, feeling as low as I did, the answer was as plain as the bloodied nose on my face: no one.

Chapter 18
Two Cool Cats

One lunchtime in September 2010, I arrived at Angel tube to be greeted by a woman called Davika. She was a ticket attendant and had been one of our most loyal friends since Bob and I had started working in Islington. She often brought Bob a little treat or something to drink, especially during hot weather. Today, however, she simply wanted to deliver a message.

'Hi, James, there was someone here looking for you and Bob,' she said. 'He was a reporter from one of the local papers. He asked me to call him back if you were willing to talk to him.'

It wasn't the first time someone had paid us attention. There were a couple of films on the internet about me and Bob that had been viewed by a few thousand people and a couple of London bloggers had written nice things about us, but no one from the newspapers had shown any interest. To be honest, I took it with a pinch of salt.

A couple of days later, however, I found this guy outside the Angel tube station waiting for us.

'Hi, James, my name is Peter,' he said.

'I was wondering if I could do an interview with you for the *Islington Tribune*?'

He took a picture of Bob perched on my shoulders with the Angel tube station sign behind us. I felt a bit self-conscious. I hadn't exactly dressed up for the occasion and had a thick, early winter's beard, but he seemed happy enough with the results.

We then had a bit of a chat about my past and how Bob and I had met.

'Great,' he said, when he'd finished asking questions. 'The article will appear in the next edition of the *Tribune*.'

I didn't really take it too seriously. I'd believe it when I saw it. It was easier thinking that way.

A few days later, Rita and Lee, the co-ordinators at *The Big Issue* stall on Islington Green, called me over.

'Hey, James, you and Bob are in the paper today,' Rita said, producing a copy of the *Tribune*.

Sure enough there was a half-page article on us written by Peter Gruner. The headline read:

TWO COOL CATS . . .
THE BIG ISSUE SELLER
AND A STRAY CALLED BOB

The story began:

Not since the legendary Dick Whittington has a man and his cat become such unlikely celebrities on the streets of Islington. *The Big Issue* seller James Bowen and his docile ginger cat Bob, who go everywhere together, have been attracting comments since they first appeared outside Angel tube station. The story of how they met – widely reported in blogs on the internet – is one of such extraordinary pathos that it seems only a matter of time before we get a Hollywood film.

I had to laugh out loud. Dick Whittington? Hollywood film? And I wasn't terribly pleased with the way I looked in the photo, sporting that thick beard. But it was a lovely piece, I had to admit.

I popped into the newsagent's and grabbed a few copies to take home. Bob did a kind of double take when he saw the picture. For a split second he had this slightly baffled expression on his face. It was as if he was saying, *No, it can't be. Can it? Really?*

In the days that followed the article, more and more people started saying hello to us, not only at Angel, but on the bus and on the street.

One morning I was taking Bob to do his business on Islington Green when a group of schoolchildren appeared in front of us. They could only have been about nine or ten years old and were in very smart, blue uniforms.

'Look, it's Bob,' a boy said, pointing excitedly.

'Who's Bob?' said one of his friends.

'That cat there on that man's shoulders. He's famous. My mum says he looks like Garfield,' the boy said.

I was touched but I thought the comparison with Garfield, the world's best-known cartoon cat, was unfair. Garfield was obsessed with eating and very lazy. Bob had always been in good shape, ate pretty sensibly and had the friendliest, most laid-back attitude of any cat I'd ever met. And no one could ever call him work-shy.

Our most significant encounter, however, came from someone I'd spoken to once before.

I was approached one evening by an American lady.

'My name's Mary,' she said, 'and I am a literary agent. I live nearby and have noticed you outside the tube station many times. Have you considered writing a book about your life with Bob?'

I said I would think about it, but I hadn't taken her seriously. How could I? I was a recovering drug addict who was struggling to survive selling *The Big Issue*. I didn't write a diary. I didn't even write texts on my mobile phone. Yes, I loved to read, and consumed all the books I could lay my hands on. But *writing* a book was about as realistic as building myself a space rocket.

Fortunately, Mary had persisted, and we'd spoken again.

'Why don't you meet with a writer who is experienced at helping people tell their stories?' she suggested, guessing my concerns. 'I know the right guy. He's busy at the moment, but I'll fix for him to come and see you soon.'

After the *Islington Tribune* piece Mary contacted me again.

'Are you happy to meet this writer I have in mind?' she asked. 'If he thinks there is a book in Bob and you, he will spend time with you, getting you to tell your story. He'll help to shape it up and write it. Then I'll try and sell it to a publisher.'

Again, it sounded too far-fetched for words.

I didn't hear anything for a while. Then, towards the end of November, I got a call from this writer guy. His name was Garry.

I agreed to meet him and he took me for a coffee in the Design Centre across the road from my pitch. We had Bob with us, so we had to sit outdoors in the biting cold. Bob was a better judge of character than me, so I made a point of going to the toilet and leaving them alone a couple of times. They got on famously, which I took to be a good omen.

I could tell Garry was trying to work out whether my story was suitable for a book. As we spoke, he said something that struck a chord.

'I can see that Bob and you were both broken souls,' he said. 'You came together when you were both at rock bottom. You helped mend each other's lives. That's the story you have to tell.'

I had never thought of it in those terms. Instinctively, I knew that Bob had been a hugely positive force in my life. I'd even seen that there was a video on YouTube that someone had filmed of me where I said that Bob had saved my life. I guessed that, to some extent, it was true. But I just couldn't imagine *that* being a story that would interest anyone.

Even when I had seen Garry again for another, longer chat, it all seemed a bit of a pipe dream. There were so many ifs and maybes. If Garry and Mary were willing to work with me, maybe a publisher would be interested in releasing a book. I really couldn't see all three of those things happening. As the festive season and the end of the year loomed into view, I told myself there was more chance of Father Christmas being real.

During the run up to Christmas, Bob and I were given a host of presents. Bob's favourite was an advent calendar filled with treats. He quickly learned to make a fuss first thing in the morning when it was time for me to produce the latest snack on the countdown to Christmas.

We also got a fantastic Santa Paws outfit. Belle had made me one for our very first Christmas together but it had somehow got lost. This one had a snug red jacket and a very striking red hat for Bob to wear during the festive season. Passers-by at Angel were besotted by it.

On Christmas Day itself Bob spent more time playing with the wrapping paper than his actual presents. I left him to it and spent the afternoon watching television and playing video games. Belle popped round for a few hours too. It felt like a real family Christmas to me.

A couple of weeks into the New Year I got a phone call from Mary.

'A major London publisher, Hodder & Stoughton, want to meet you, James,' she said. 'And Bob, of course.'

A few days later, we went along to their offices in a rather grand tower block near Tottenham Court Road. At first, the security people wouldn't let Bob into the building. They looked baffled when we said he was going to be the subject of a book. I could see their point. What on earth would Hodder be doing publishing a book about a scruffy-looking bloke and his ginger tom cat?

In the end, Bob was treated like visiting royalty. He was given a goodie bag with some little snacks and catnip toys and allowed to explore the offices. Wherever he went he was greeted like some kind of celebrity. People were snapping away on their phones and cooing over him.

'I knew you had star quality, Bob,' I told him with a laugh, 'but I didn't realise it would be quite this good.'

I, on the other hand, had to sit in a

long meeting, talking about everything from marketing and publicity to production and sales. The long and the short of it was that they had seen some of the material Garry and I had worked on and they wanted to publish a book based on it. Between them, they'd even come up with a title: *A Street Cat Named Bob*.

'Come and visit my literary agency in Chelsea,' Mary suggested.

Again, it was a very grand and slightly intimidating place. There were a few odd looks when people realised that a *The Big Issue* seller and his cat had walked in. While Bob explored the offices, Mary ran me through the contract that I'd been offered by the publishers.

'It's a good deal,' she said, 'especially as you're an unknown author.'

I placed my trust in her and signed all

the paperwork. It felt weird scrawling my name, but also very, very exciting. This couldn't really be happening. Not to me.

Chapter 19

Start at the Beginning

I began meeting Garry once or twice a week in Islington. This suited me really well because it meant that I could top up my money by spending a few hours working afterwards. But it also meant that I had Bob with me. This meant that finding somewhere to sit and talk was a challenge, especially when the weather was bad. The local cafés wouldn't let a cat on the premises and there wasn't a library nearby. So we had to find alternatives.

The first people to invite us in from the cold were Waterstones, the bookshop on Islington Green. They knew me in there. I'd often popped in with Bob to look through the Science Fiction section. The manager there, Alan, was on duty one day when I was with Garry.

'Do you mind us working upstairs in a quiet corner?' I asked him.

He not only said yes, he got a member of staff to organise two chairs for us in the History section. He even brought a couple of coffees in.

Garry and I were determined that the book wouldn't just be about my life with Bob. We wanted it to offer people some insights into life on the streets. I wanted to show how easy it was for people like me to fall through the cracks, to become forgotten and overlooked by society. Of course, in order to do that, I had to tell my 'back story' as well.

I wasn't looking forward to that part. Talking about myself wasn't something that came easily to me, especially when it came to the darker stuff. But once we began talking, to my surprise, it was less painful than I'd feared. It forced me to confront some painful truths and helped me to understand myself a little better.

I knew I wasn't the easiest person to deal with. I had a defiant, self-destructive streak that had consistently got me into trouble. I'd always tried really hard to fit in and be popular as a kid, but it had never worked. I'd ended up trying too hard – and become a misfit and an outcast as a result.

On a happier note, I had some wonderful people helping me at the time and I remembered how I had wanted to give something back so had begun donating boxes of comic books to a hospital I'd gone to. I'd managed to get myself some work experience in a comic book shop nearby and persuaded the boss to let me take boxes of unsold magazines for the other kids there. I'd spent many hours playing air hockey and watching video games in the activity room they had in the children's ward so I knew they'd all appreciate something decent to read.

In the main, however, I didn't have great memories of being a child.

I knew I couldn't blame the doctors, my mother or anyone else for the way my life had gone since then. I made mistakes

of my own free will. I hadn't needed anyone's help to screw up my life – I'd done a
perfectly good job of that on my own.

If nothing else, the book was an opportunity for me to make that crystal clear.

When I showed him the cheque I'd been
given for the book, my dad was lost for
words. The expression on his face was a
mixture of disbelief, happiness, pride –
and mild apprehension.

'That's a lot of money, Jamie,' he said
after a couple of moments. 'You'd better
be careful with that.'

The reality hadn't really sunk in until
now. Not just for my dad, but for me
either. There had been meetings with
publishers, contracts signed, even articles

in the newspapers. But it hadn't been until I received this cheque for the advance that it finally struck home.

When it had first flopped through the letterbox a couple of days earlier, I had opened the envelope and then simply sat there looking at it. The only cheques I'd seen in the past decade had been for small amounts, £50 here and £100 there, never anything with more than a couple of noughts on it.

Compared to some people, especially in London, it wasn't actually that large a sum of money. For a lot of the commuters walking past me each day on their way to the City of London, I guess it wasn't even a month's salary. But for me, it was an eyewatering amount of cash.

The arrival of the cheque, though, had brought two immediate problems. I was terrified of frittering it away. But I also didn't have a bank account into which I could pay it. Which was why I'd travelled to my father's house in south London.

'I was hoping you could look after it for me,' I asked him over the phone. 'I can then ask you for money as and when I need it.'

Dad agreed. Rather than meeting as usual at Victoria, he'd invited me over to his neck of the woods. We went for a couple of drinks in his local and chatted for a couple of hours.

'So is this going to be a proper book?' he asked me.

'What do you mean?'

'Well, is it a picture book or a children's book? What is it going to be about exactly?' he said.

'It's the story of how I met Bob,' I explained, 'and how we helped each other.'

He looked a little nonplussed. 'So will me and your mother be in it?' he asked.

'You might get a mention,' I said. 'But don't worry. The only person that comes out badly in all this is me.'

That made him change tack a little.

'Is this going to be a long-term thing?' he continued. 'You writing books?'

'No,' I said, honestly. 'I'm not going to become the next J.K. Rowling, Dad. There are thousands of books published every year. Only a tiny minority of them become bestsellers. I really don't think a tale about a busker and his stray ginger cat is going to be one of them. It's a nice windfall, but no more.'

'All the more reason to be careful with the money then,' he said.

He was right, of course. But when he went off into a lecture about various investments and savings schemes, I tuned out completely.

Chapter 20
Fun and Trouble

Being with Bob has been such an education. He has taught me as much, if not more, than any human I've come across. I've learned important lessons about everything from responsibility and friendship to selflessness. He has even given me an insight into a subject I thought I'd never really understand – parenthood.

Caring for Bob has made me realise that parenthood is all about anxiety. Whether it is fretting over his health, watching out for him when we are out on the streets, or simply making sure he is warm and well fed, life with Bob often feels like one worry after another.

It actually chimes with something that my father had said to me after we'd lost contact for a time. It had been at the height of my addiction, and both he and my mother had been beside themselves with concern about me.

'You have no idea how much a parent worries about his or her child,' he had shouted at me. 'It's so selfish, not getting in touch with us.'

It hadn't meant much to me then. But since being with Bob, I have come to understand what he meant. I wish I could turn back the clock and save them all that grief.

That is the bad news. The good news is that 'parenthood' brings a lot of laughter with it too. For far too long I'd found it hard to find much joy in life. Bob has taught me how to be happy again. Even the slightest, silliest moments we share together can bring an instant smile to my face.

One Saturday lunchtime, for instance, I answered a knock on the door and found the guy from the flat across the hallway standing there.

'Hi,' he said. 'I just thought I'd let you know that your cat is out here.'

'Must be someone else's. Mine's in here,' I said, turning around to scout around the living room. 'Bob. Where are you?'

There was no sign of him.

'No, I'm pretty sure this is him out here. Ginger, isn't he?' the guy said.

I stepped out into the hallway to discover Bob sitting perfectly still on top of a cupboard on the landing, with his head pressed against the window, looking down on the street below.

'He's been there a while. I noticed him earlier,' the guy said, heading for the lift.

Bob looked at me as if I was the world's biggest party pooper. The expression on his face seemed to say: *Come on up here and take a look at this view with me, it's really interesting*.

Belle was visiting and was in the kitchen rustling up a sandwich.

'Did you let Bob out?' I asked. 'I can't work out how he got out into the hallway and hid himself up on top of the cupboard.'

'I popped downstairs about an hour ago to put some rubbish out,' Belle said, remembering. 'He must have slid out without me noticing, and then hidden away somewhere when I came back up. I'd love to know what's going on in his mind sometimes.'

I couldn't help laughing out loud. I'd wondered the same thing on many occasions.

There was nothing Bob loved more than watching the world go by. He would regularly sit on the kitchen win- dowsill, monitoring the goings on below, like some kind of security guard.

His head would follow people as they walked towards and then past our block of flats. If someone turned into the entrance to the building, he'd stretch his neck until he lost sight of them. I found it incredibly entertaining. It was almost as if he had a list of people who were allowed to travel this way at certain times and in certain directions.

He'd see someone passing and look as if to say, *Yes, OK, I know who you are,* or, *Come on, you're running late for the bus to work.* At other times he'd get quite agitated, as if he was thinking: *Oi, hang on! I don't recognise you!* or *You don't have clearance, where do you think you're going? Get back here.*

Bob loved playing hide-and-seek too. I'd found him hiding in all sorts of surprising nooks and crannies. He particularly loved anywhere warm.

One evening, I went to have a bath before I went to bed. As I nudged the bathroom door open, I couldn't help thinking it felt a little odd. Rather than swinging open easily it needed an extra nudge. It felt heavy somehow.

I didn't think much more of it and started running a bath. I was looking in the mirror by the sink when I noticed something moving on the back of the door amongst the towels I kept in a rack. It was Bob.

'How on earth have you got up there?' I said, howling with laughter.

I worked out that he must have climbed on to a shelving unit near the door and then jumped on to the towels. It looked pretty uncomfortable as well as precarious, but he seemed really happy.

Another frequent trick was to hide inside the clotheshorse I often used to dry my washing in the bathtub, especially during winter.

Several times I'd been in the bathroom and suddenly noticed the clothes moving. Bob would push the clothes apart like curtains, his face wearing a sort of *peek-a-boo* expression. He thought it was great entertainment.

Bob's antics often got him into trouble.

He loved watching television and computer screens. He could while away endless hours watching wildlife programmes or horse racing. So when we walked past the gleaming new Apple store in Covent Garden one afternoon, I thought I'd give him a treat. The place was bursting with shiny new laptops and desktops, none of which I could afford. But the Apple philosophy was that anyone could stroll in and play with their technology. So we did.

We had spent a few minutes playing with the computers, surfing the internet and watching YouTube videos when Bob spotted a screen that had a kind of aquarium-style display, with exotic and really colourful fish swimming around. I could see why he was attracted to it. It was absolutely stunning.

I took him over to the giant screen and let him gape at it for a few moments. It was funny to watch. He would follow a particular fish as it moved across the screen and then disappeared. He would then do a sort of double take and dart behind the giant screen, expecting to find the fish there. Then he'd dart back again and start following another fish.

It carried on like this for a few

minutes until I turned around to see his paw wrapped around a white cable. He was pulling on it and was threatening to drag one of the giant consoles with him.

'Oh, Bob, what are you doing?' I said.

A couple of Apple 'geniuses' were standing there laughing.

'He's a star, isn't he?' one of them said.

'If he breaks anything, I'm afraid you'd have to cover the costs,' said a more senior member of the team.

Given the prices of the products on display in the store, I wasted no time in untangling him and getting out of there.

Chapter 21
The Joy of Bob

When Bob and I first got together, he didn't like going down the escalators and lifts on the underground and especially hated the crowds there during the rush hour. Over the years, however, he has conquered his fears ... and now it has become somewhere he likes to misbehave! He even has his own travelcard, given to him by the staff at Angel tube station.

Now he travels just like any other Londoner, going about his or her business. He trots along the tunnels, always walking close to the wall for security. When we get to the platform, he stands behind the yellow line, unflustered when the train pulls into the station, despite the noise it makes. He then waits patiently for the doors to slide open before padding quietly on board and checking for an empty seat.

Even the most ice-hearted commuters melt when they see him sitting there. They snap away with their camera phones, then head off to work smiling. Living in London can be tough. The idea that we are somehow lightening people's days cheers me up.

Travelling on the tube has its perils, however.

One evening we'd headed home from

central London on the tube to Seven Sisters, the nearest tube station to my flat. As we were coming up the escalator, I noticed Bob's tail was sticky and coated in a black, tar-like material. The stuff was on his body too.

I was at a loss to know what it was exactly. It looked like engine oil or some sort of heavy grease. But I did know that it was potentially harmful.

Bob seemed to have worked this out as well. He'd spotted the mess and had already decided that giving it a lick wasn't a good idea.

My phone was low on credit but I had just about enough to make a call. I rang a friend, Rosemary, a vet who had helped us out once before when Bob had been ill. She loved Bob and was always willing to help.

'Bob is covered in some kind of engine oil,' I told her. 'What should I do?'

'You need to wash it off right away,' she advised. 'Motor and engine oil can be highly toxic to cats. It can cause really bad inflammation and burning of organs, especially the lungs. It can also cause breathing problems, seizure and even death in really bad cases.'

'You're scaring me,' I said, feeling uneasy.

'You really need to wash it off him,' she repeated. 'If it doesn't come off, you should take him to the Blue Cross or another vet first thing in the morning. Does Bob let you bathe him?'

Cats seem to fall into two categories when it comes to bath time: there are those who hate it and those who love it. Luckily, Bob falls well and truly into the second camp. In fact, he is a bit obsessed with his bath.

He loves nothing more than climbing into the tub when I run a bath. He has learned that I always run a warm bath rather than a steaming hot one and hops into the tub so that he can paddle around in it for a few minutes.

It is funny – and, of course, very cute – to watch him walking around afterwards as he lifts and shakes one paw at a time.

He also gets very possessive about the bath plug and steals and hides it. I end up using a makeshift plug, only to find the real plug lying on the living room floor where Bob has been playing with it.

Sometimes I have to put a jug with a weight on it over the plug to stop him from stealing and hiding it.

So given all that, it was no problem getting him into the bath so that I could get this mystery grease off his tail.

I didn't have to hold him down. I used both hands to rub his tail and his side using some cat-friendly shower gel. I then hosed him down with the shower head. The expression on his face was hilarious: a mix of a grimace and a grin. Finally I dried him with a towel. He loved it and was purring throughout.

I popped into the Blue Cross at Islington later that week and got them to give him a quick check up, just in case. They told me there was nothing to worry about.

'Easier said than done,' I said to the nurse. 'There's always something to fret about with this one.'

I realised afterwards that I sounded a little like a parent.

In the years since we'd found each other, Bob had become domesticated — but only to a certain degree. When it came down to it, he remained a stray cat at heart.

My gut feeling is that he must have spent a large part of his young life living off his wits on the streets. He is a Londoner, born and bred, and is never happier than when he is exploring it. I often smile to myself and say, 'You can take the cat out of the street, but you can't take the street out of the cat.'

Bob has a few favourite haunts. At Angel, he loves visiting Islington Memorial Green, the little park where he is free to rummage around in the bushes, sniffing out whatever catches his interest while he does his business. There are a few overgrown corners where he can discreetly disappear for a few moments of privacy. Not that privacy bothers him too much.

He is also very fond of the grounds of St Giles in the Fields churchyard just off Tottenham Court Road. Often, when we walk from our bus stop on Tottenham Court Road towards Neal Street and Covent Garden, he starts moving around on my shoulder.

I want to stop at St Giles, he seems to tell me. *I want to check it out.*

The graveyard at St Giles is an oasis in the middle of one of the busiest parts of the city, with benches to sit and watch the world go by. For some reason, Bob's favourite toilet spot there is in full view of the street, by a set of railings on a wall. He is unfazed by the flood of Londoners passing by and often quietly goes about his business there.

When we were working on Neal Street, Bob's preferred toilet spot was outside an office block on Endell Street. It was overlooked by several floors of conference rooms and offices, so, again, wasn't exactly the most private spot in London. But Bob felt comfortable there and always managed to squeeze himself into the shrubbery so that he could get on with things as quickly and efficiently as possible.

Like all cats, he's very methodical about toileting. He digs himself a decent-sized hole, places himself over it while he does the necessary, then starts scrabbling dirt to cover up the evidence. He always levels it off afterwards so that no one would know it was there. I wonder why cats do this? I read somewhere that it's a territorial thing.

The gardens in Soho Square were another favourite stop-off if we were working in that area. Dogs were banned, which meant I could relax a little more if I let Bob off the leash too. Bob was fascinated by birds and Soho Square park was filled with them. He would sit there, wide-eyed, staring at them, making a curious little noise.

Raa, raa, raa.

It sounded really cute, although it was probably quite sinister. Scientists think cats mimic eating when they see potential prey. In other words, they are practising chomping them to bits in their mouth when they catch them!

Bob loves nothing more than chasing mice and rats and other creatures when I let him loose in parks. One day, I was reading a comic book in Soho Square when he arrived with part of a rat's head dangling from his mouth.

'Bob, that's going to make you really sick,' I said.

I don't think he had any intention of eating it. Instead he took it into a corner and started playing with it. Ninety-nine times out of a hundred Bob draws admiring glances from passers-by. On that particular occasion, a few people looked at him in utter horror.

I had never been one of those cat owners who saw their pets as little angels. Far from it. Like all members of his species, Bob is a highly effective predator. If we had been living in other parts of the world, I'd have been more concerned. In parts of the USA, Australia and New Zealand, they have tried to ban cats being allowed out after dark. They claim domestic cats are doing so much damage that birdlife in particular is being endangered. This wasn't such a problem in London. As far as I was concerned, Bob was free to do what came naturally to him, as long as he didn't risk hurting or harming himself.

Apart from anything else, it is great entertainment, for him – and for me.

One day, for instance, we were looking after Titch's dog Princess again. I decided to take Bob and Princess to a small park near the flats where I live.

I was sitting on a bench with Bob on the extra-long lead I'd made for him when he suddenly spotted a grey squirrel.

Princess spotted it too. Soon the pair of them were bounding towards it. The squirrel, quite sensibly, scampered up the nearest tree, but Bob and Princess weren't deterred.

I watched them as they worked together, trying to work out how to flush the squirrel out of the tree.

Princess would bark every now and again to try and rattle the squirrel. Every time the squirrel appeared or made a move, the two would adjust their positions. Bob was covering one side, while Princess was covering the squirrel's other potential escape route at the back of the tree.

They carried on with this for twenty minutes before eventually giving up.

I'm sure some people must have thought that I was ever-so-slightly mad because I sat there giggling away, engrossed by every captivating minute of it.

Chapter 22
Public Enemy No. 1

Another summer was on its way and the midday sun was already blazing as Bob and I settled down in a shady spot outside Angel tube station. I had just got out a bowl and filled it with some water for Bob when I saw two men approaching.

'Hello there, sir. We're police officers, and members of the Community

Safety Unit for Islington. Can you tell me your name?' the older of them asked me.

'Erm, it's James Bowen. Why?'

'Mr Bowen, I'm afraid we have had an allegation of assault made against you. We are going to have to ask you to accompany us to the police station to answer a few questions,' the younger guy said. 'It shouldn't take us more than a few minutes.'

I was surprised at how calm I was. In the past I'd have started panicking. It was a measure of how much more con-trolled and together I was these days, since having Bob. Besides, I hadn't done anything wrong; I was just helping them with their enquiries.

My mind was churning as we walked to the police station, trying to work out who might have made this 'allegation'. I had a few thoughts already.

The most obvious explanation was that someone was just trying to muck up my day. Sadly, it was pretty common. Sometimes someone selling *The Big Issue* would do it simply to get the person away from their pitch and then claim it for themselves. I'd made the Angel tube pitch a success, and I knew several people would love to have taken it over. It wasn't nice, but it was a fact of life.

The other possibility was that someone was trying to undermine my book. By now pretty much everyone in *The Big Issue* community knew about it. More newspapers had picked up on the story and several vendors had made comments, positive and negative.

Some vendors thought that I shouldn't

be allowed to sell the magazine any more. Stupidly, I'd imagined that I was doing something positive for the magazine. Instead, it felt like I'd turned into every vendor's Public Enemy No. 1.

By the time we got to the station, both of the police officers were on first name terms with Bob. They seemed really smitten with him.

'Right, let's get Bob settled before we take you into the custody suite,' the older officer said.

We were soon joined by a blonde, uniformed female PC in her late twenties. Bob seemed to take an instant shine to her and was soon rubbing his face on her hand, purring away as he did so.

'Do you think he'd mind if I picked him up?' she said.

'Go for it,' I said, sensing that he was already at ease with her.

As I suspected, he let her scoop him up.

'Why don't you come with me, Bob, and we can see if we can sort you out with something nice to eat or drink?' she said.

I watched as she took Bob behind the main reception desk to an office area with desks and photocopiers and fax machines. Bob was fascinated by all the red lights and buzzing machines and was happy in there. So I left him there as I headed off with the officers.

'Don't worry, he's safe with Gillian,' the younger officer said to me as we went through a set of doors into the custody suite. I felt certain he was telling the truth.

I walked into an interview room with the police officer, who sat me down and asked me some questions.

'Were you near this address in Islington yesterday?'

'I'd like to help you, but I honestly don't know what you are talking about,' I said.

After about ten minutes, or less, we were done.

'OK, Mr Bowen, we'll need you to stay here for a bit while we look into this further,' the younger officer said.

I was impatient to be reunited with Bob and to get back to work though. When a duty PC offered me a cup of tea in the interview room, I asked about Bob.

'It's OK, he's with Gillian still downstairs,' he said. 'He's a pretty happy chappie down there.'

Eventually, the two officers came back into the interview room.

'I'm afraid I think we've wasted your time and our time,' they said. 'The person who made this accusation on the phone hasn't been willing to come down to give a formal statement. So there's no evidence against you and so there will be no charges.'

I was both relieved and angry. But there was no point in complaining, especially as everyone had been so decent. My main concern once more was Bob. What had they done with him for all this time?

I had to go down to the reception area to sign out. Bob was there with Gillian, looking as content as when I'd left him. But the moment he saw me his tail started swishing and his ears perked up. He leaped into my arms.

'Gosh, someone's pleased to see you,' Gillian said.

'Has he been a good boy?' I asked her.

'He's been a star. Haven't you, Bob?' she said. 'I popped out to the shops and bought him some cat milk, a pouch of meaty food and a packet of treats.'

No wonder he was so happy, I thought.

'In normal circumstances he'd have been placed with any stray dogs that were being held,' Gillian told me. 'If you'd been kept in overnight, we'd have had to think about putting him there. But luckily that won't be necessary now.'

By the time I had left the station it was getting towards sunset. All day I'd been worrying about someone stealing my pitch, so I headed back to Angel just to check. To my relief, there was no one there.

'You all right, James?' one of the flower sellers asked me.

'Yeah, just someone's idea of a joke,' I said a little bitterly. 'Reporting me for assault.'

'What's wrong with people?' he said, shaking his head in disgust.

It was a good question.

About a week later, Bob and I were selling magazines during the rush hour when an attractive, blonde lady came up to us. Bob seemed to recognise her and arched his head towards her when she kneeled down beside him.

'You don't remember me, do you?' she said to me as she made a fuss of Bob. 'Tolpuddle Street station? I was the one who looked after Bob the other week.'

'Oh, yes, of course. Sorry,' I said, genuinely mortified. 'It's Gillian, isn't it?'

'Looks like you are both doing well,' she said. 'We didn't really have much of a chance to talk when you were at the station the other day, for obvious reasons. So how did you two get together?'

She smiled and laughed out loud a couple of times as I recounted our early days together.

'Soul mates by the sound of it,' she said.

She could tell that I was busy and that the rush hour was about to begin so was soon on her way.

'I might pop by and see you again if that's all right,' she said.

'Sure,' I said.

She was true to her word and was

soon stopping by to see us regularly, often bringing gifts for Bob. He seemed to have a genuine soft spot for her.

Gillian was generous to me as well. On one occasion she brought me a coffee, a sandwich and a cookie from one of the local coffee shops. We chatted for a little while. I explained to her what was happening to us with the book and how it seemed to have generated more animosity than anything else.

'Ah, don't worry about that. People are always jealous of others' success. It sounds great,' she said. 'Your friends and family must be so proud of you.'

'Yeah, they are,' I said, giving her a sheepish smile.

The truth was that I didn't have many friends. Aside from Belle, there was no one to whom I could turn – in the good times or the bad times. I had Bob and that was about it.

It was, in part, the life that I'd made for myself. I was a product of the environment in which I'd spent the past decade. But even now that I was clean, I found it hard to establish friendships. I found it hard to trust people. The events of the past couple of weeks had underlined that. For all I knew the person who had falsely accused me could have been someone I saw every day of the week. It could have been someone I regarded as a 'friend'.

So as I looked at Bob interacting with Gillian, a part of me wished my life could be as simple and straightforward as his. He had met her in strange circumstances but had immediately sensed he could trust her. He knew that she was a decent person and so he had embraced her as a friend.

I knew it wasn't going to be easy, but I needed to take that same leap of faith. To do that, however, I had to change my life. I had to get off the streets.

Chapter 23
Pride and Prejudice

It was the first Saturday of July and the streets of central London were packed for the annual Gay Pride celebrations. The hot weather had drawn even more revellers than usual. According to the news, a million people had come out to watch the huge parade of floats filled with dancers and spectacular costumes snake its way from Oxford Circus, down Regent Street to Trafalgar Square.

I'd decided to kill two birds with one stone, and had spent the day watching the floats and fabulous outfits while also selling a few magazines at a pitch on Oxford Street near Oxford Circus tube station.

It was a valuable day for all *The Big Issue* sellers so, as a 'visitor' from Islington, I had been careful to make sure I stayed within the rules. I was also careful not to 'float': the term used to describe selling whilst walking around the streets. I'd fallen foul of that rule in the past and didn't want to do so again.

This year the crowds for Gay Pride were packed four or five deep in places, but everyone was in an incredibly good mood, including Bob.

He'd got used to being in big crowds. There had been a time when he had a slight phobia of people in really scary outfits, but his years of walking the streets of London seemed to have eased his fears. He'd seen everything from weird, silver-painted human statues and French fire-eaters to giant dragons during Chinese New Year.

Today, there was no shortage of outrageous outfits and people blowing horns and whistles. Bob took it all in his stride. He sat on my shoulders, soaking up the party atmosphere and loving the attention he was getting from the huge crowds. Quite a few people knew him by name and asked to have their picture taken with the pair of us. One or two even said they were looking forward to reading about us in our book.

'We need to write it first,' I half joked.

As the main parade drew to an end late in the afternoon, Bob and I headed towards Soho Square, when I felt a tap on my shoulder. I turned around to see an outreach worker called Holly.

'James. You're floating,' she said.

'No, I'm not,' I protested.

'You were floating, James. I saw you,' she said, adamant. 'I'm going to have to report you.'

I decided that Holly wasn't going to spoil my day and carried on enjoying the party atmosphere.

The following Wednesday, the trouble began.

Arriving in Islington just before

midday, I went to see Rita, the co-ordi-nator on Islington Green, to buy new supplies of magazines.

'Sorry, James,' she said. 'I can't sell you any. Apparently someone saw you floating in the West End. You know the drill. You've got to go over to Head Office in Vauxhall.'

It was infuriating for all sorts of rea-sons. First and foremost, of course, it was a complete nonsense to say I'd been floating. Secondly it was a real bore having to travel over to Vauxhall. But I knew I had to keep my pitch at Angel going. The book was just a passing phase; I knew I couldn't turn my back on what was still my bread and butter.

At *The Big Issue* office, I had to sit around for half an hour before I could see a supervisor.

'I'm afraid you are going to have to serve a one-month suspension because an outreach worker saw you floating,' he said.

I tried to defend myself but nothing helped. So I decided to take it on the chin and accept the suspension. I signed the paperwork, handed in my tabard and ID card and headed home, upset but resigned.

'That's just the way the cookie crumbles, Bob,' I sighed. 'What's that saying? No good deed goes unpunished.'

I decided to spend the month working on the book and doing a little busking. At the end of the month, I went back to *The Big Issue* office and got my tabard and ID back. I also bought a supply of magazines to take back to Angel.

'Back to business, Bob,' I said as we

caught a bus and headed back across the Thames.

Arriving back at Angel, I emerged from the station and saw my pitch was empty. So I set up as normal and got back to work.

I'd been there for about half an hour when another vendor arrived. He was a guy I'd seen around occasionally. He was relatively new to *The Big Issue* and had a rather scruffy and bad-tempered old dog.

'What are you doing? This is my pitch,' he said.

'No, it's not,' I said, looking bemused. 'This has been my pitch for more than a year now.'

'It might have been your pitch a year ago, but it's mine now,' he said. 'Go and talk to Rita. She'll fill you in.'

'I will, mate, don't you worry about that,' I said, marching straight across the High Street towards the co-ordinator's spot on Islington Green.

It was obvious immediately that something was wrong because Rita's face crumpled when she saw me.

'Oh, hi, James,' she said, refusing to make eye contact. 'Someone in Vauxhall went over my head. They told that guy he could have the pitch full-time. There was nothing I could do.'

I was lost for words.

It may sound boastful, but I made that pitch really successful. Until I arrived, no one had wanted to work there. Everyone thought people were in too much of a hurry to slow down at that spot, that they didn't have time to talk to a vendor and buy a magazine. But, largely thanks to Bob, of course, I had established myself there. Even the outreach workers had said that the number of people who came to see us was amazing. As were sales of the magazine.

'I can't believe they've done this to me,' I said to Rita. 'Is it because I've got this book deal and they assume I don't need to sell any more? Because if it is they've got it all wrong. That's only a flash in the pan. I need to keep working long-term.'

But Rita just kept shaking her head and saying, 'I don't know,' or 'I'm sorry.'

In the end I just stormed off, with Bob on my shoulders.

I am not proud of what I did next, but I felt so cheated and badly treated that I decided to take matters into my own hands.

I headed back to the tube station and confronted the guy again.

'Here's £20 for the pitch. How's that?' I said.

He pondered it for a moment then grabbed the note, picked up his magazines and headed off with his dog in tow.

I had barely been there ten minutes when he arrived back, this time with Holly.

'James, this isn't your pitch any more,' she said.

'Yes, it is. I just paid the guy £20 to get it back,' I said.

'It doesn't work that way and you know it, James,' she said.

I couldn't understand why they were doing this to me. Had I behaved so badly? Was I that unpopular amongst *The Big Issue* fraternity? I must have been. They all seemed to have it in for me.

'So can I have my £20 back?' I said to the guy.

'No. I haven't earned anything yet,' he said.

I could see that he hadn't bought any magazines, so he couldn't have spent the £20. I lost it this time and started busking about twenty feet away. I wasn't allowed to, but I didn't care.

Holly reappeared with a police officer and another outreach worker, John, in tow.

'I'm afraid I'm going to have to ask you to move on, sir. Otherwise I will have no option but to caution you,' the PC said.

'You're going to get another suspension for this, James,' Holly said.

Enough was enough. I decided that I would end my association with *The Big Issue*. I didn't feel great about it. Selling the magazine had done wonders for me. But I just felt a deep sense of injustice.

I had probably over-reacted and lost my temper when I'd discovered my pitch had been given away. I just felt betrayed, especially because Bob and I had become unofficial ambassadors for the magazine. I'd been in the *Islington Tribune* a couple of times and the *Camden Journal*. The *Independent* had even published a piece. Each and every one of them mentioned that I was selling *The Big Issue*. It was the kind of feel-good coverage the magazine wanted. We embodied the ethos of the charity: they had helped us to help ourselves. Or at least, so I thought.

Once again, I began to wonder

whether the high profile Bob and I were winning was a double-edged sword. But I knew what I had to do.

I didn't go to Vauxhall to sign my six-month suspension. As far as I was concerned, I'd sold my last copy of the magazine. I was sick of it all, and it was bringing out the worst in me.

From now on I needed to concentrate on Bob, the book and all the things that brought out the best in me instead.

Chapter 24
The One That Saves Me

The drama at Angel left me feeling lost for a little while. Deep down I knew I'd done the right thing, but I still had my moments when I worried that I'd made a bad move.

It took me a week or so to snap out of it.

'You can't dwell on it forever,' I told myself. 'You have to move on and, in particular, you have to focus on the positives, especially the book.'

For a week or two after Garry and I handed in the manuscript, I half expected a phone call saying, 'Sorry, we've made a terrible mistake.' But that didn't happen.

'We're going to publish it next spring, in March,' they told me.

I now had a target to aim for. In the meantime I had to keep earning money, so I headed back to busking – and to Covent Garden.

I had mixed feelings about this. After a couple of years selling *The Big Issue*, it felt like a little bit of a backward step. My voice had deteriorated too. Shouting out, 'Big Issue! Big Issue!' hundreds of times a day was more demanding on my voice than singing a tuneful song. Playing the guitar again took some

getting used to as well. I didn't have cal-
louses on my fingers for a start.

But there were some positives too. I
tried to focus on them.

Most significantly, it was a step
towards independence. *The Big Issue* had,
without question, been a force for good
in my life. It had helped me find a little
stability. Without them I would probably never have been asked to write a
book. But I'd found it hard to abide by
their rules. I wasn't very good at dealing
with authority. I never had been.

So being my own person again felt
good. I'd got my freedom back.

Of course, the other really positive
thing was that Bob and I were better
known now. Thanks to the various
pieces in newspapers and on the internet, we were minor local celebrities.

From the first day busking, it was clear to me that we were now drawing bigger crowds than previously. There would be times when little semicircles of tourists and shoppers would surround us, snapping away with their cameras and kneeling down to stroke Bob. I was shocked at how many people that I didn't even recognise would smile, point and say: 'Aaaah, Bob.' Bob seemed to relish it.

One of the most requested songs I played was 'Wonderwall' by Oasis. I'd played it a hundred times, but now, each time I played those familiar chords, the lyrics hit home much harder. In particular, that line in the chorus that goes: *'Maybe you're gonna be the one that saves me'.* As I looked down at Bob, I realised it could have been written for him. There was no maybe about it. He had saved me.

Another positive about being in Covent Garden, of course, was that life was never dull. The place had a rhythm and life all of its own. The busiest time of the day was the evening rush, around 7pm, when people headed home from work and even more flooded in to visit the bars, restaurants, theatres and opera houses.

You could easily spot the kids who were out for a night's clubbing. They were all mini-skirts and towering heels, leather jackets and hair gel. The opera lovers were the best dressed, often with the men in black tie and the women in grand evening dresses with plenty of bling. The area was full of characters. As we settled back into the busking routine, we seemed to attract more than our fair share of them once more.

One afternoon, a couple of weeks into summer, I noticed an unfamiliar face on the pavement a few yards away from us.

It wasn't uncommon for other people to set up in the area, trying to earn a few quid. I didn't have any problem with that, as long as they didn't interfere with our livelihood.

This guy was dark skinned and dressed quite smartly, in a suit. He had an odd-looking basket, which he placed on the floor. I guessed he was some kind of street entertainer, but I had no idea what to expect.

I sat there watching him for a few moments, hoping he might ease the boredom of another day. I wasn't disappointed. He had soon dipped into his basket and produced a yellowish snake which he draped around his neck. I was no expert on snakes, but I'd have described it as an albino python. It was quite thick and about three feet long. He then started playing around with it, asking for donations from passers-by.

'Look, Bob, we've got a snake charmer,' I smiled as I watched the impressive-looking creature coiling its way around the guy.

It was obvious Bob didn't really understand what was happening. We were a good thirty feet away so he couldn't really see properly, he settled back into his favourite position in the shade and started his afternoon snooze.

The guy had been there for about forty minutes or so when he came over to say hello. He still had the snake draped on his neck like a large piece of jewellery.

'OK, guys, how are you today?' he said, in a strong accent that I guessed was Portuguese or possibly Brazilian.

Bob had been dozing away in the afternoon sun but perked up and took a good look at the curious visitor. I could tell his mind was hard at work, trying to work out what this creature was and whether it was a welcome presence. It didn't take him long to reach his conclusion.

As Bob tilted his head forward to take a better look, the snake decided to stick out its long, forked tongue and deliver a rather scary hiss. It was like something out of *The Jungle Book*.

Bob completely freaked.

Mrow! he yowled, and jumped up at me imploring me to stick him on my shoulders. I was pretty sure that if he hadn't had his harness on he would have bolted.

'Sorry, dude, didn't mean to scare your cat,' the guy said, realising what he'd done and sliding the snake off his shoulders. 'I'm going to move away from here and see how I get on further down the road.'

Bob spent the rest of the afternoon on edge. He was so paranoid about meeting another snake that he kept attacking the straps on my rucksack. He'd been sitting on this rucksack for years and had never had a problem. But suddenly anything that reminded him of the yellow python was treated with suspicion. He kept grabbing the straps in his teeth and flicking them in the air, as if to test whether they were alive or not.

It took Bob a few days to get over the snake. It must have been confusing for him. For all these years, he'd been the only creature that rode around the streets, draped across a man's neck. I think it completely threw him to see another creature there, especially such an alien one.

Of course it was all part of being back in the wacky world of Covent Garden.

Not everyone on the streets was so understanding though. It remained a competitive and sometimes aggressive place, full of people only looking after No. 1.

Bob and I were happily whiling away an afternoon on Neal Street when a young guy pitched up with an amplifier and a microphone. He was dressed in skater-boy clothes and was wearing a baseball cap and Nike trainers. All he had was a microphone.

I ignored him and got back to playing my own music.

I wasn't able to shut him out of my mind for long though. Within minutes I heard an ear-splitting, repetitive noise booming out. He was strutting around with his mic against his lips, beat-boxing. I'm a fan of most forms of music but this really wasn't my cup of tea. As far as I was concerned it was just noise.

Bob made his opinion of this 'music' plain immediately. He cast his eyes down the street with complete disdain. Then he stood up, tilted his head at me and let me know in no uncertain terms that we should move.

I gathered my stuff and moved about seventy yards down the street where I began playing again. I could still hear the din from the young kid, but at least I could hear myself think.

Others must have complained because within half an hour or so a police van arrived. I saw the boy waving his arms around in protest at the police officers, but it didn't get him anywhere. After a couple of minutes I saw him disconnect his microphone and start to pack up.

You could almost hear the sighs of relief that must have been breathed in the offices, cafés and restaurants.

'Thank goodness that's over, eh, Bob?' I said.

My joy was short-lived.

'You're not licensed to play here, mate,' one of the police officers said, noticing me and Bob sitting there.

I decided not to push it. Easing myself

back into life in Covent Garden was difficult enough without aggravating the police. *Choose your battles, James*, I told myself. Wisely, as it turned out.

Chapter 25
An Inspector Calls

It was just after midday on Neal Street in Covent Garden and the crowds of tourists and shoppers were beginning to thicken. I'd barely got myself set up and started playing when I saw a lady in a ribbed blue jumper and trousers walking towards me. I could tell she was not a tourist. As she drew close, I saw that her jumper had epaulettes and badges and had a familiar logo on it. She was from the RSPCA: the Royal Society for the Prevention of Cruelty to Animals.

The RSPCA do a great job in preventing animal cruelty and promoting animal welfare, and had been a huge help to me and Bob in the past. Today, I got the distinct impression that their presence wasn't going to be good news.

'Hello, James, how are you today?' the lady said, producing a card with her ID on it. It showed that she was an inspector.

I was a bit thrown by the fact that she knew my name.

'Fine, thanks. What's the problem?'

'I've been asked to come and see you because I'm afraid we have had complaints that you are mistreating your cat, Bob, isn't it?' she said.

I was horrified. Who had complained? And what had they said I was doing to Bob? I felt physically sick for a moment, but knew I had to keep my wits about me in case this got serious.

'I'm sure they are unfounded allegations. I can see that you treat Bob well,' she said, giving him a little tickle under the chin. 'But I do need to have a chat with you and then examine him to make sure there's nothing wrong.'

It wasn't the first time people had accused me of mistreating Bob, of course. The complaints generally fell into three categories. The first was that I was exploiting him for my own benefit. My answer to that argument was always the same: a cat is never, ever going to do something it doesn't want to do. And it is never going to be with someone it doesn't want to be with, no matter what that person does to it. Bob was a very strong character, with a free will of his own. He wouldn't have hung around if he didn't trust and like me. And it was his choice whether he wanted to come out with me each day.

There were still days when he didn't fancy taking to the streets. They were rare, to be honest. He genuinely enjoyed being out and about, meeting people and being fussed over. But when he hid away or refused to follow me out the door I always respected his decision. There would always be those who wouldn't believe that, of course, but it was the truth.

The second common accusation was that I was mistreating him by having him on a lead. If I'd had a pound for every time I'd heard someone say, 'Oh, you shouldn't have him on a leash, he's a cat not a dog,' I'd have been a very rich man. I'd explained so many times that it was to keep him safe, I was bored at hearing myself say the words. But, again, I could keep saying it until I was blue in the face as far as some people were concerned. For them it was an open-and-shut case: I was some kind of animal-abusing monster.

The third and most upsetting allegation was that I was drugging Bob. I'd only heard that a couple of times, thankfully. It cut me to the quick both times. Given what I'd been through in the past ten years and the battle I'd fought to kick my drug habit, I found that the most hurtful insult of all.

The RSPCA inspector took out a

microchip reading device to check that Bob was microchipped, which he was, of course. The device showed up my name and address as Bob's legal owner.

'That's a good start,' she smiled. 'You'd be surprised how many cat owners don't chip their pets, even these days.'

She then checked his fur for fleas, took a look at his teeth and checked his breath, perhaps to see if there was anything wrong with his liver or maybe his kidneys. She also checked his eyes to see if they were cloudy. That made me wonder whether someone *had* tried to accuse me of drugging him. It made my blood boil to think someone would say that to the RSPCA.

I had to be positive, I told myself. I hadn't done anything wrong.

'Has Bob got any health problems that

you are aware of, James?' the inspector asked me, her pen poised over her notebook.

'No,' I said. 'I regularly take him to the weekly drop-in Blue Cross clinic in Islington. They always praise me for the way I look after him. They've not spotted anything so I think he's pretty healthy.'

'That's good to know, James,' she said. 'So tell me, how did you two get together in the first place?'

I told her the story and she nodded and smiled throughout.

'Sounds like you were meant to be together,' she laughed. 'He's a fine fellow, isn't he? Don't suppose you have a phone number that I can reach you on?'

My battered old mobile phone was still working – just – so I gave her the number.

'I'm happy for now,' she said, 'but I may need to follow up with another visit. Are you here every day?'

'Yeah, pretty much,' I said, already feeling uneasy.

'OK, I will give you a call or drop in to see you soon.'

She then gave Bob a final ruffle and headed off into the crowds.

On the one hand I was pleased that she had left without any major drama. But I was still worried. I knew the RSPCA had significant powers when it came to pet owners. Why was she doing a follow-up visit? What was she going to tell her superiors? What if I was prosecuted and, heaven forbid, Bob was taken away from me? I couldn't help all these things going through my head.

You're overthinking things, don't worry, I told myself.

As I headed home that evening, however, I still had a knot of anxiety in my stomach. I had an awful feeling that this was going to hang over me for a while.

About a week later the RSPCA inspector appeared again. She was a lot friendlier and more relaxed this time. Bob responded well to her as she kneeled down to check how he was doing. Again, she made some notes and asked me a couple of questions about what we'd been up to that week and what we had planned in the coming days.

Then she watched us interacting together and with the passers-by.

RSPCA inspectors are obviously trained to read animal behaviours. She could see that Bob was perfectly content to be there and to be doing his little stunts for his audience.

'I'll be in touch very soon,' she said as she left, giving Bob another friendly stroke and shaking my hand with a smile.

I carried on for an hour or so, but my heart wasn't in it. I was about to pack up when I saw the housing manager of one of the blocks of flats on Neal Street striding over. We'd clashed before over my busking. She had obviously been watching from a window and had seen the RSPCA officer shaking my hand and walking off.

'People are trying to sleep upstairs,' she said.

'It's two o'clock in the afternoon,' I said, genuinely baffled.

'Never mind that,' she said as if I was some three-year-old child. 'You shouldn't be busking here. Can't you read the sign?' And she pointed at a plaque across the road.

'But I'm not busking on that side of the road, I'm busking here,' I said. 'And I am entitled to do that if I want.'

But she obviously wasn't interested in having a debate about it.

'I've had enough of you and that cat. I'm going to call the police and have you removed,' she said, marching off.

Her argument seemed ridiculous to me. How on earth could I disturb people from their sleep in the middle of the afternoon? If anything was going to wake up her residents, it was the constant din of delivery vans and lorries and police sirens. It was crazy.

About half an hour later, I saw a police van drawing into the street a hundred yards or so away from our pitch.

'I don't like the look of that, Bob,' I said, unstrapping my guitar and packing up.

By the time two policemen had walked over, I was ready to leave.

'You have to move on,' they said.

'Yes, I know. I'm off,' I said.

The incident had really riled me. I became convinced that this lady was the one who had reported me to the RSPCA.

Back at the flat that evening, the RSPCA inspector rang me on my mobile.

'You have absolutely nothing to worry about,' she said. 'Bob's a special creature and you're doing a grand job. My advice to you is to ignore those who tell you any different.'

It was the wisest advice I'd had for a long time. And, unusually for me, I took it.

Chapter 26
Doctor Bob

I was finding it harder and harder to haul myself out of bed in the morning. For the past few weeks I'd actually grown to dread the sight of the late winter sun, leaking light through my bedroom window.

It wasn't that I didn't want to get up. I wasn't sleeping well and was usually awake by first light in any case. My reasons for wanting to hide under the duvet were very different. I knew that the moment I got up, I would just start coughing again.

I'd suffered from chest problems for some time, but recently they had got really bad. No sooner had I got up in the morning than my lungs and chest were filling up with phlegm and I was coughing really violently. At times it was so bad that I was doubling up in pain and I would begin retching and vomiting. It was awful.

I was getting really worried about it. I had tried to get rid of the coughing by dosing myself with cheap medicines from the supermarket. But it had got me nowhere.

'Take a few paracetamol and get some rest,' advised one doctor I saw. But that hadn't achieved much at all.

Bob sensed I was unwell and started paying me attention. He would wrap himself around me as if taking some kind of measurements. I'd learned the lessons of the past and didn't dismiss him this time.

'Here comes Doctor Bob,' I joked one day.

There was no question in my mind that Bob was performing some kind of diagnosis. When I was lying on the sofa or on the bed, he would often spread himself out on my chest, purring gently.

I'd read somewhere about cats having the power to heal bones with their purring. I wondered whether he was trying to somehow heal my chest. More worryingly, I wondered whether he knew something I didn't.

In a way, that was the scariest thing of

all. I knew how accurate cats could be when it comes to sniffing out illness in humans. One cat I read about, from Yorkshire, would give its owner 'strange looks' before he was about to have a fit. Famously, there was a cat called Oscar who lived in an old people's home in America and would come and sit with residents who were in their final hours. Oscar's ability to anticipate people's passing was uncanny, so much so that people dreaded seeing him sidling up to them. I hoped Bob wasn't doing something similar to me!

After a while I made another appointment at my local clinic, this time with a young doctor that a friend had recommended to me. He certainly seemed sympathetic. I told him about the coughing and the vomiting.

'I'd better take a listen to your lungs,' he said.

After checking me out with a stethoscope, he tested my breathing and chest. I'd had childhood asthma so I knew my chest was weak. He didn't say too much. He just sat there making notes. Rather too many of them for my liking.

'OK, Mr Bowen, I'd like you to have a chest X-ray,' he said. 'Take this form along to the hospital and they'll know what to do.'

There was something about his face that spooked me a little. I didn't like it.

I took the form home and stuck it on the sideboard in the front room. I then quietly forgot about it. A small part of me couldn't face the hassle. It wasn't that long ago that I'd been hospitalised with DVT. What if I had to be admitted

287

again? What if it was something even worse? I really didn't like hospitals. I told myself that I couldn't afford to waste a day there, not earning money.

Of course, these were all excuses. The truth was that I was terrified of what an X-ray might find. It was pure stubbornness. I assumed that if I stuck my head in the sand and forgot all about it, the coughing and vomiting and all the other unpleasantness would simply go away. Of course it didn't. It only got worse.

I reached breaking point one day when I visited my book publishers. I had, at last, begun to believe that the book was finally happening. They'd mocked up a cover, with Bob sitting Zen-like on my rucksack. On the back was a picture of me, while inside was a brief note on 'the author'. I still had to pinch myself to believe it was happening.

Unfortunately, I had a coughing fit in the middle of the meeting.

'I need the toilet,' I gasped, and dashed off there.

I knew it must have looked pretty bad and that I couldn't repeat it in March. Publication was looming and I'd been told that I might be doing a few media interviews, even an appearance on television. There was also talk of book signings where I'd meet members of the public. It all seemed pretty far-fetched, but to be on the safe side I decided I had to get to the bottom of this and go for the X-ray.

I knew that, this time, I couldn't really duck out of it.

I went along to hospital and was led

into a large room. A nurse placed a big metal plate on my chest before moving behind a screen to take the X-ray.

'How did it look?' I asked the nurse, fishing for a clue.

'Fine,' she said. 'But we will send a full report to your doctor. Should be there in a few days.'

So I waited a few days then received a phone call to say I should head to my doctor's for the results. I went along with a real sense of foreboding.

I have a tendency to think the worst, as you will know by now, so I was braced to hear something terrible. I was slightly taken aback when the doctor looked at the notes attached to his copy of the X-ray images and said, 'Your lungs are completely clear, Mr Bowen.'

'Really?' I said.

'Yes. There's not a single black spot, you seem to have super healthy lungs.'

'So why am I coughing my guts up all the time?' I asked, confused.

'I suspect you've got an infection of some kind,' he said, prescribing me some heavy-duty antibiotics.

'That's it?' I said, relieved but slightly shocked to discover it was that simple.

'Well, let's see if they work,' he said. 'If not we will have to explore things a bit more.'

I was sceptical. It couldn't be that simple, I told myself. But it was. Within days my chest was feeling much better and the coughing was easing off.

My agent, Mary, had been worried about my health. She'd been anxious that the publicity and the signings that would soon be coming up might be too much for me. I knew that she had my best interests at heart.

'You seem a lot better,' she told me when we met for a chat about the publication of the book which was now just weeks away.

But it was when I got another opinion that I really knew I was in the clear.

I was lying on the bed reading a comic book. Out of nowhere, Bob appeared and jumped up. He slid up to me in the same way he had done over the previous few weeks, placing himself on my chest and purring quietly away. After a moment or two, he put his ear to my chest, doing his feline stethoscope act. He lay there for a moment, listening intently. And then, as quickly as he'd arrived, he'd gone. He just picked himself up and hopped off the bed in the direction of his favourite radiator. I couldn't help smiling.

'Thanks, Doctor Bob,' I said.

Chapter 27
A Famous Face

There is a saying that March comes in like a lion and goes out like a lamb. They were right about the first bit. There were days when the wind blowing down the alleyways of Soho and the West End made such a raw, rasping noise it could almost have been a lion's roar. Some days I struggled to feel the tips of my fingers as I played my guitar.

Fortunately, Bob was better insulated than me.

Even now, with spring around the corner, Bob still had his luxurious winter coat. His tummy was also still carrying some of the extra weight he'd put on over Christmas. The cold hardly seemed to bother him at all.

Bob and I missed Angel, but if I was honest, we were enjoying life more in Covent Garden.

We'd become a double act and seemed somehow more at home amongst the jugglers and fire-eaters, human statues and other street performers that roamed the Piazza and surrounding streets. It was a competitive place, of course, so, as we settled back into daily life in central London, we polished up our act.

Sometimes I would play my guitar

while sitting cross-legged on the pavement with him. Bob always loved that and would drape himself across the body of my guitar. We'd shake hands and he'd stand on his hind legs to collect treats. We also had a new party piece.

It had started back at the flat one day while Bob had been playing with Belle. As usual, he was tossing his shabby old Scraggedy Mouse around. Belle wanted to take it off him so that she could give it a decent wash.

'It needs a good scrubbing, Bob,' I heard her telling him. 'You can have a treat if you give it to me.'

Choosing between his Scraggedy Mouse and the treat was a real dilemma. Bob dithered for a second before going for the treat. He released the mouse from his jaws long enough to receive the little snack – and for Belle to whisk the toy from under his nose.

'Well done, Bob,' she said. 'Give me five.'

And she put her hand in the air like an American footballer or basketball player, inviting his teammates to celebrate a score.

I saw Bob raise his paw to give her an acknowledgement.

'That was cool,' I laughed. 'Bet you can't get him to do it again.'

'Bet I can,' Belle said, and did.

Since then Bob had come to associate giving a 'high five' with receiving a treat. On Neal Street it had pulled in all sorts of admirers, including some rather famous ones.

It was around 4pm on a Saturday afternoon and a couple of little girls had stopped to admire Bob. They were about nine or ten years old and were accompanied by a small group of adults, including a couple of big, burly bouncer-like guys in dark glasses. To judge by the way they were surveying the scene while the girls stroked Bob, they must have been security minders.

'Daddy, look at this,' one of the girls said excitedly.

'Oh yeah. That's a cool cat,' a voice said.

I froze to the spot. I recognised the voice immediately.

'It can't be,' I said. But it was.

Standing behind me was the unmistakeable figure of Sir Paul McCartney.

I wouldn't have expected one of the greatest figures in popular music of all time to talk to me. He was in a slightly different league to me when it came to knocking out a tune. But he seemed charming.

I had my early edition of the book alongside me on the floor and saw it catch his eye. I also had a wad of flyers advertising the first book signing the publishers had organised in three days' time.

Inside my head a little voice was saying, *Oh, go on, give him one.*

'Erm, I've written a book about me and Bob,' I told him, motioning to my ginger companion sitting at my feet. 'I'm having a signing next week if you want to come along,' I said, handing him the flyer.

To my amazement he took it.

People were flashing away with their cameras. For once it wasn't Bob they were snapping.

'We'd better move along kids,' the lady with him said. I worked out that she was his new wife, Nancy Shevell. She seemed really cool.

'Take care man and keep it going,' Sir Paul said.

I was slightly starstruck afterwards and on Cloud Nine.

There wasn't a chance of Sir Paul McCartney coming along to the signing. Why would he come? But that really didn't matter now. The book had already allowed me to achieve the impossible. I'd chatted to a member of The Beatles.

Later that afternoon, before heading home, I sat down on the pavement to give Bob a couple of treats. Tomorrow was the day of the book signing in Islington. I wanted to get an early night, although I knew I wouldn't sleep much. I also didn't want to keep Bob out for much longer as it was getting cold.

As I stroked him, I noticed immediately that his body language was very defensive. His back was arched and his body was stiff. He wasn't interested in the treats either. Instead, his eyes were fixed on something in the near distance. Something – or someone – was clearly bothering him.

I looked across the street and saw a rough-looking character staring at us.

Living your life on the streets, you develop an radar when it comes to people. I could spot a bad apple instantly and this guy looked rotten to the core. It was obvious that he was working out how to steal my money.

Bob and I had probably collected £20 in the space of half an hour. I knew better than to leave too much money on display and had slipped most of it into my rucksack. He'd obviously registered this.

I decided not to confront him. As long as he kept his distance, there was no need. Just to make sure, however, I looked across at him and nodded, as if to say: 'I've spotted you, and I know what you're thinking. So just forget about it.'

Street people speak the same language. We can convey a hundred words with a simple look or expression. He understood me immediately. He just growled, got up and slinked off.

The instant the guy disappeared around the corner, Bob relaxed.

'Don't worry, mate,' I said, slipping a little snack into his mouth. 'He's gone on his way. We won't see him again.'

Chapter 28
Cat to the Rescue!

We'd had quite a day, and had soon collected more than enough to get Bob and me a few days' worth of shopping, so I decided to head home.

Bob needed to do his business before we got the bus, so we headed for his regular spot outside the posh office block on Endell Street.

I was halfway down the street when I

felt Bob moving on my shoulders. At first I thought he was simply dying to go to the toilet.

'Hold on for another second, mate,' I said. 'We're almost there.'

But I soon realised he was just taking up a new position. Unusually, he had turned to face backwards rather than forwards.

'What's wrong, Bob?' I said, turning around.

The coast seemed clear enough to me. Bob didn't seem quite so convinced. Something was definitely bothering him.

I'd barely taken a dozen steps when all of a sudden he made the loudest noise I'd ever heard him make.

Wheeeeeow! Hsssssssss!

At the same time I felt a tug on my rucksack and then an almighty scream.

Aaargh!

I swung round to see the bloke who had been staring at us earlier on Neal Street. He was bent over double with huge scratches on the back of his hand. Blood was gushing from his wounds.

It was obvious what had happened. The guy had made a lunge for my rucksack and Bob must have lashed out with his claws. He'd dug them deep into this guy's hand, ripping into the skin. Bob was still in fighting mood too. He was standing on my shoulders, snarling and hissing.

'Look what your cat's done to my hand!' the guy shouted, waving his bleeding arm at me in the gloom.

'Serves you right, you were going to mug me,' I said.

Bob was screeching and hissing at him more animatedly than ever.

Wheeeeeeooooow! Hsssss! Hsssss!

The guy turned on his heels and stumbled off into the gloom, still holding his hand.

On the bus back home, Bob sat on my lap. He was purring steadily and had tucked his head under my arm, as he often did when he – or I – felt vulnerable. I guessed we were both feeling that way after our encounter, but I couldn't be sure, of course.

'Cats are mysterious kind of folk – there is more passing in their minds than we are aware of,' Sir Walter Scott wrote. In many ways, that was part of Bob's magic. We had been through so much together, yet he still had the ability to startle and surprise me. He'd done it again this evening.

We'd never been attacked like that.

And I'd never seen him react and defend me in that way either. I'd not been switched on to the threat this guy posed at all, but Bob had.

How had he sensed the guy was not to be trusted? And how had he detected his presence when we were walking away from Neal Street? I'd seen no sign of him anywhere. Had Bob caught a glimpse of him hiding in an alleyway? Had he smelled him?

I didn't know. I would never truly know what went on in Bob's brain. Yes, we were best friends. We had an almost telepathic bond. But that understanding didn't mean we could share our deepest thoughts. We couldn't really tell each other what we felt. As silly as it sounded, I often felt sad about that. And I did so now.

Holding him close to me as the bus lurched its way through the London traffic, I had an overwhelming urge to know what Bob had felt back there in the side street. Had he been scared? Or had he fallen back on his instincts and just dealt with it in the moment? Had he already forgotten about it, or was he thinking the same kind of thoughts as me? *I am fed up with this life. I am sick of having to look over my shoulder all the time. I want to live in a safer, gentler, happier world.*

I suspected I knew the answer. Of course he'd rather not be fighting off scumbags on the streets. Of course, he'd rather be sitting somewhere warm rather than freezing on a pavement. What creature wouldn't?

As my mind ticked over, I dipped into my pocket and pulled out a scrunched-up flyer. It was my last one. I'd given the rest away. It had a photo of me with Bob on my shoulders and read:

Come and meet
James Bowen and Bob the cat
James and Bob will be signing
copies of their new book

A STREET CAT NAMED BOB

at Waterstones,
Islington Green, London
on
Tuesday 13th March 2012 at 6pm

Bob looked at it and tilted his head. I was sure that he recognised us.

I stared at the scrap of paper for what must have been a couple of minutes, lost in my thoughts.

How many more times would I have to put myself and Bob in the firing line? Would I ever break this cycle and get us off the streets?

I flattened the flyer out neatly and folded it away in my pocket.

'I hope this is the answer, Bob,' I said. 'I really do.'

Chapter 29
Waiting for Bob

It was barely 9am but my stomach was already churning away like a cement mixer. If I felt like this now how on earth was I going to feel in nine hours' time?

Waterstones in Islington was the obvious venue for the book signing. The store was part of my story in more ways than one. Not only had the staff there helped us when Garry and I were writing the book, they even featured in one of the more dramatic scenes where I'd run in the front door, desperate and panic-stricken, when Bob had run off after being scared by an aggressive dog at Angel tube station.

In the days running up to the event, I started giving interviews to more newspapers but also for radio and television. To help me get used to this, I was sent to a specialist media trainer in central London. He taught me a few tricks of the trade. During one of the first recordings, for instance, I'd fiddled with a pen while talking. When it was played back to me, all I could hear was the sound of me tapping the pen against the desk like some manic rock drummer. It was incredibly distracting and annoying.

'People will want to know how you ended up on the streets,' the trainer told me. 'You need to be prepared for questions about how Bob helped change your life and what the future holds for you both.'

'Fine,' I said, a little nervously.

'You'll also have questions about whether you're clean of drugs,' he warned me.

'I'm happy to do that,' I said. I felt I had nothing to hide.

The signing was scheduled two days ahead of the official publication date, March 15th, which also happened to be my 33rd birthday.

I hoped that wasn't going to put a hex on everything. Birthdays hadn't been much fun for me, certainly not since my teens.

I spent my thirteenth birthday in a children's ward at the Princess Margaret Hospital for Children in Western Australia. It was a miserable time in my young life. Not long afterwards I started sniffing glue and experimenting with marijuana. It was the start of my long descent into drug addiction.

I couldn't help but look back on all my previous birthdays, what I was doing at 13 and 23, and how different my life had become.

Ten years further down the road, my life had finally taken a positive turn. When I looked back now, I found it hard to believe that I'd lived through that period. But, for good or bad, it would always be a part of me. It was certainly a part of the book. I'd decided not to sugarcoat my story, which was another one of the reasons I felt so racked with nerves.

In the hours before the signing, Bob and I were filmed by a photographer from the Reuters international news agency. He wanted to take a series of photos of us travelling around on the tube and busking on Neal Street. I was glad of the distraction.

By the time we finished, it was early evening. A damp chill was beginning to descend when we got back to Islington and made the familiar walk from Angel tube station.

There was no sign of the guy who had 'acquired' my pitch outside the tube station.

'That guy and his dog caused all sorts of trouble,' a flower seller told me when I asked about it. 'There's no one from

The Big Issue selling magazines outside Angel any more.'

'What a waste,' I said. 'I built that pitch up into a nice earner for someone.'

But that wasn't my concern any more. I had other things to worry about.

Bob and I walked through Islington Memorial Green towards Waterstones. We were early so I let Bob do his business and sat on the bench to enjoy a few quiet moments. Though I was nervous I was also really excited. A new chapter in my life was beginning.

I had so many conflicting thoughts fighting for space in my head. What if no one turned up? What if loads of people turned up and thought the book was rubbish? How would Bob react if there was a crowd? How would people react to me? I wasn't a typical author. I was a guy who was still operating on the fringes of society. Or at least, that's how it felt.

Luckily Bob was being extra cool for both of us. He spent a couple of minutes rooting around in a favourite little spot then sauntered back to me. He just gave me a look.

It's all right, mate, it's all good, he seemed to say.

It was uncanny how he was able to calm me.

Arriving at the bookshop about half an hour before the signing was due to start, there were four or five people standing in line outside.

Ah well, someone has turned up at least, I said to myself, relieved.

They all smiled at us and I gave them

a sheepish wave. I couldn't quite get my head round the idea that people were giving up an hour of their evening to come and meet us. There were a few more people inside the store as well. They were all stood in a queue to pay and were all holding copies of the book.

'Come upstairs to the staffroom,' said Alan, the manager. 'You can have a drink and Bob can have a saucer of milk. You can take it easy for a minute before things get under way.'

Belle, Mary, Garry and a bunch of people from the publishers were in the staffroom to wish me luck. There was also a stack of books for me to sign for general sale in the store. Someone had come up with the bright idea of having a paw-shaped stamp so that Bob could also 'sign' each book. I got to work

scrawling on the first copies. Belle added
the final flourishing touch with the paw
stamps. There were at least two dozen
books in the pile. Were they sure they'd
even sell this many?

At one point a member of staff arrived,
beaming.

'It's stretching all the way around the
block,' she smiled.

'What is?' I said, stupidly.

'The queue. It's stretching all the way
back around the corner. There's probably a hundred people there with more
joining all the time.'

I was speechless. For a moment, I
thought about climbing out of the open
window, shimmying my way down the
drainpipes and making a hasty escape!

The clock ticked down towards 6pm.
Bob climbed up on my shoulders and we

headed back downstairs to the shop floor. I took a sneaky look down and my heart jumped into my throat. It was heaving with people.

A table stacked with books had been laid out ready for me and Bob. The line of people was stretching along the bookshelves all the way to the entrance and out into the dark March evening. They were right. There must have been a hundred people and more in it. At the other side of the store, a separate queue of people were lined up, buying copies of the book. There was even a group of photographers and a television cameraman there.

As we started walking down the final flight of steps, the cameras began flashing and photographers began shouting,

'Bob, Bob, this way, Bob.'

There was even a ripple of applause and a couple of cheers.

My years on the street with Bob had taught me to expect the unexpected. But this was totally uncharted territory.

One thing was clear: we'd come too far to pass on this chance.

'Come on, Bob,' I whispered, stroking the back of his neck before taking a final, deep breath. 'No turning back now.'

Epilogue
Always

That night in March 2012 was probably the most important of my life. The book signing in Islington was a success way beyond my expectations. Paul McCartney didn't quite make it, but more than three hundred other people did. The numbers caught everyone by surprise, even the bookshop, who were cleaned out of every one of their two hundred or so copies within half an hour.

'So much for my prediction that we'd only sell half a dozen,' I joked with Alan, the store manager, after three hours of signing and interviews.

When *A Street Cat Named Bob* went on general sale two days later it became what *The Times* described as 'an instantly bestselling memoir'. It entered the bestseller list on the first weekend after publication – and remained in the UK bestseller list for the best part of a year, most of that time at No. 1.

Each Sunday, I would pick up a newspaper and look at the latest chart, shaking my head slowly. Why was it so popular? What had captured the public's imagination? After a while I gave up trying to work it out and just enjoyed it.

The book swiftly found a foreign audience too. In Italy it was *A Spasso Con Bob (A Walk with Bob)*. In Portugal it was *Minha História Com Bob (My Story with Bob)*. Whatever the language, people seemed to love the story. Most of all, of course, they simply adored Bob.

Bob and I appeared on television and radio programmes to talk about the book and its popularity. For our first major appearance on the BBC's *Breakfast* programme, I was a bundle of nerves, paranoid that Bob would be scared of the lights or the strange surroundings. But he sat happily on the sofa watching himself on the monitors in front of him. He even did a series of high fives for the hosts who seemed to be every bit as bewitched by him as everyone else. He was the star of the show.

Wherever we went I was asked the same questions. In particular, people would ask how the success of the book was changing life for the both of us.

It took a little while for the financial rewards of the book's success to trickle in, so for a few months we continued to busk on Neal Street. Gradually, however, we were able to reduce our appearances. It was such a huge relief to wake up each morning knowing we wouldn't have to face the cold and the rain. Knowing that I wouldn't have to experience that sense of uncertainty and quiet desperation that I felt when I used to set off for Angel or Covent Garden was life changing.

A small part of us would always remain there of course. We continued to make occasional appearances, but now we were doing it in order to help other people rather than ourselves.

At the beginning of 2013, for instance, we formed a relationship with the animal charity, Blue Cross. We raised almost £5,000 for them in the first week and by the end of the year had increased that to more than £20,000. It felt fantastic to be able to give something back. They were so kind to me during my early days with Bob, and continued to help us when we popped into their weekly clinics on Islington Green.

I'd often felt that Bob was my reward for some act of kindness that I'd shown someone earlier in my life. I'd felt like it was karma. By helping the Blue Cross, I felt like I was returning their generosity, performing another act of karma. I aim to do the same thing for homeless charities at some point in the future.

'Has the book made you rich?' people ask.

Well, I didn't become an overnight millionaire, but at least I knew I didn't have to scour the shelves of supermarkets for 10p tins of past-the-sell-by-date baked beans. For the first time in many years, I had a bank account and even an accountant. I had to pay taxes for the first time in more than a decade.

When you are homeless or selling *The Big Issue* you know you aren't contributing to society and that part of society resents you for that. A lot of people take great pleasure in telling you, 'Get a job, you scrounger!'

People don't always understand the general hopelessness you feel when you

are homeless, busking or even selling
The Big Issue. Paying my taxes made me
feel that I was once more 'a member' of
society. And it felt good.

There were so many other positives to
the book's success.

It improved my relationship with my
parents. The bewildered but delighted
look on my father's face when he saw the
queues at that first Waterstones signing
will live in my memory for a very, very
long time. After all the disappointments,
I felt like I'd given him something to be
proud about. At last.

Apparently he shed a tear when he
read the book back at home. He called
me up to say well done, and said the
same thing again on other occasions.
He still told me to get a haircut and a
shave, of course, but at least he stopped

nagging me to 'get a proper job'.

I also travelled to Australia again to spend time with my mother. She'd read the book and wept when reading it as well. We were able to be open and honest with each other and realised that we'd be friends from now onwards.

Another satisfying aspect of the book's success was the impact it seemed to have on people's attitude to *The Big Issue* sellers and the homeless in general. Schools and charities wrote, telling me how our story had helped them to better understand the plight of the homeless.

Bob and I were also on Facebook and Twitter. Every day it seemed we got a message from someone explaining how they no longer walked past *The Big Issue* vendors but stopped and bought a magazine. Many told me they now made a point of talking to them too. I felt a huge sense of pride in that. *The Big Issue* is a fine institution that deserves everyone's support, especially in these dark economic times.

Our story also seemed to connect with people who were facing difficult times in their lives. Some read our story of survival and drew their own strength from it. Others recognised the power animals possess to heal us humans. Again, I was immensely proud every time I received a message of this kind. I never in a million years expected that I'd touch the life of one person, let alone thousands.

A few people got a little carried away and called me and Bob 'saints'. Bob might have been a saint but I wasn't, that was for sure. You can't live a chunk of your life with the problems that I had without being damaged by your experiences. In short, Saint James of Tottenham didn't exist. He never had and he never would.

The person who did exist, however, was someone who had been given his second chance in life and was determined to seize it.

I recently received a letter from a lady in a small, rural community in Wales whose close friend had just lost her long fight against cancer. The lady had given our book to her friend during her final days. She had been so touched by it that she had, in turn, given a copy to her local Minister. During her friend's funeral in the small village chapel, the Minister had held up a copy of our book.

'This book meant a great deal to the lady at the end of her life,' he'd told the congregation. 'Bob and James are an example of the power of faith, hope and love.'

Reading this moved me to floods of tears. It was unbelievably humbling. It remained in my head for days.

Those three precious qualities – faith, hope and love – had been missing in my life for a long time. But then all three came along in the mischievous, playful, occasionally grumpy but always devoted cat who helped me turn my life around.

Bob had helped me restore my faith in myself and the world around me. He had shown me hope when I really couldn't see much of it. Most of all he had given me the unconditional love each of us needed.

During one of my television appearances on the BBC, a presenter asked me a question which threw me at first.

'What will you do when Bob is not around any more?' he asked.

I got a little emotional at the very thought of losing him, but once I'd gathered myself, I answered as honestly as I could.

'I know that animals don't live as long as us humans,' I said, 'but I will cherish every single day that I share with him. And when the time comes for him to leave, he will live on in the books that he inspired.'

They may have been the truest words I ever uttered.

The world as it was before I met Bob seemed a harsh, heartless and, yes, a hopeless place. The world I have grown to see through his eyes is very different. I am happier, healthier and more fulfilled than I have ever been. I have escaped my life on the streets. I can see a clear path ahead of me. If it had not been for the love of Bob none of this would have happened, I am sure.

I have no idea where our adventure will lead us next. But I know that, for as long as he is around, he will be at the heart of it all. He is my companion, my best friend, my teacher and my soul mate. And he will remain all of those things. Always.

Acknowledgements

Writing this book has been a collaborative process and I need to thank the team of incredibly talented and supportive people who helped me cross the finishing line. Garry Jenkins was my principal guiding hand, skilfully extracting the stories then shaping the manuscript. At Hodder, I have to thank Rowena Webb and Maddy Price along with Ciara

Foley, who edited the script. I would also like to single out the brilliant publicists Emma Knight, Kerry Hood and Emilie Ferguson. A big thanks also to Dan Williams for his superb line drawings.

At Aitken Alexander I'm totally indebted to my fantastic agent Mary Pachnos as well as the team of Sally Riley, Nishta Hurry, Liv Stones and Matilda Forbes-Watson. Thanks also to Joaquim Fernandes at Aitken Alexander and Raymond Walters and his team at R Walters & Co for their invaluable guidance and help.

Closer to home I'd like to thank my best friends Kitty and Ron for being at my side through what has been a pretty crazy year or so. It hasn't been easy at times, but they've remained steadfast and loyal and I owe them more than I can say. I'd also like to thank my mother and father for their love and support, not just in the past year but throughout the darker and more difficult earlier years when I was, I know, far from the easiest of sons.

I can't let this opportunity pass without thanking the legions of people who have written to me either directly or through social media, passing on their good wishes and sharing their experiences. I've done my best to reply to as many as possible but hope that I can be forgiven for not getting back to each and every one of you. The response has been, at times, overwhelming. Most of all, of course, I'd like to thank the little guy who remains my constant companion. I still don't know whether I found Bob or

ACKNOWLEDGEMENTS

he found me. What I do know, however,
is that without him I'd be utterly lost.

James Bowen, London, May 2013

Bob Information Page

For the latest news, stories and
pictures from James and Bob,
follow them on Twitter at
www.twitter.com/streetcatbob,
or visit their Facebook page at
www.facebook.com/streetcatbob

To Mum, Dad
&
'wee' Bess,

with all my love,

Graham.

SO THIS IS GLASGOW!

SO THIS IS GLASGOW!

BY

LEMUEL SWIFT GULLIVER

GLASGOW

JACKSON, SON & COMPANY

PUBLISHERS TO THE UNIVERSITY

1938

FIRST PUBLISHED BY
JACKSON, SON & CO. (BOOKSELLERS) LTD
Publishers to the University
GLASGOW
1938

LONDON : SIMPKIN, MARSHALL & CO. LTD.

To

GLASGOW AND ITS HOSPITABLE PEOPLE

CONTENTS

CONTENTS

Chapter I BY WAY OF INTRODUCTION

My name is Lemuel Swift Gulliver. I think it better to begin with that simple statement, for there can be but few readers of what is to follow who have not heard of my famous ancestor and the record of his travels given to the world by Jonathan Swift.

Lemuel bought a little estate in Oxfordshire, where he settled after his four adventurous voyages, and generations of Gullivers lived there quietly. But some reckless speculations of my grandfather, in the eighties of last century, brought disaster to the family. The estate had to be sold, the family was scattered, and my father settled in Tasmania, where I was born, almost thirty years ago.

My father prospered in Tasmania, to such an extent that when he died—my mother predeceased him by several years—I, his only son, inherited a comfortable fortune.

Except for some distant relatives on my mother's side, I was alone in the world. I had no ties; had all the money I needed; and the world was my oyster. And so I set out on my travels, visiting Africa, India, the Americas and eventually, Europe. For some reason that was not quite clear to me, I left the country of my ancestors to the last. Although I had decided that I could never settle in any country, there must have been a feeling deep down in my being that I might, eventually, make Britain my home. So I left it to the last.

I arrived in London—having flown from Paris—and had not been there two days until I had the good fortune to meet a man who had been a fellow-passenger in the ship in which I had sailed from Australia to Africa. We became friendly on that trip, and I was quite glad to see him. He asked me to dine at his club where, by a strange turn, I was introduced to another member who had known my father in his young days. The result was that I was put up for the club, was admitted as a member, and I took a service flat in town.

London, I found, resembled most huge cities, except that it was more parochial in its outlook than a small village. Anything that happened outwith a certain radius was regarded as of no account. People who lived outside of London were known to exist, but that was all. I soon tired of this attitude of the Londoners, and what eventually set me on my travels again was their attitude towards Scotland.

Scotland, to my fellow-clubmen and to some others that I met, was a somewhat barbaric country. Some had shot in the Highlands, others had but a passing acquaintance with the North, and others again had never been there. I was amazed to hear the opinions expressed about the country and its people, for I had met not a few Scotsmen in all parts of the world, and they had impressed me as highly intelligent men.

When I ventured to say so, I was told that those were the Scots who had escaped from Scotland, and that, naturally, they were different from the inhabitants, who were hardly civilized. 'Take Glasgow, for example,' said one man. 'Even in that so-called city, honest peaceful people are afraid to go about their business. Terrible gang fights take place; wild men abound everywhere on Clydeside, and it is known that every second man carries a razor concealed about his person. I expect the people live in mud huts and subsist on pibrochs or some such outlandish dish.'

3

'But surely', I said, 'a city that has given so many fine things to the world in engineering, and has built so many fine ships; a country that has produced a Burns, a Scott, a Stevenson, a Barrie and many other fine writers, not to mention great men in all the arts and in science, cannot be what you say?'

But they merely laughed and shrugged their shoulders.

'If I were going to Scotland,' said one man, 'I'd certainly not make Glasgow my headquarters. It's a dirty and dust-filled miserable city. Give me Edinburgh every time.'

A chorus of approval greeted that remark.

So I made up my mind to see for myself. I decided to come to Glasgow with a completely open mind. My idea was to see Glasgow, its life and its people, through the eyes of a visitor from another planet as it were. In this way I would get a fresh, unbiassed view, and I would do my best to write about it simply, truthfully, and without exaggeration. I might even be able to show Glasgow to its people in a new light.

I have already told you that all my inclinations were to travel and to write about my travels, but until now my pen has been idle, except for the many notes I have made of my wanderings. Do not, therefore, I beg of you, expect a work of great literary merit. I do not strive to accomplish such a work. I shall be merely a recorder, a reporter, of the life that goes on around me in Glasgow, setting down such matters as interest me at the time of their happening. I shall set nothing down in malice, for mine is a kindly nature, looking for the best in my fellows.

I have told nobody of my intentions. I have given up my flat, packed my bags, and in a few minutes I shall be in a taxi to take me to the station. And so to Glasgow.

Chapter II

It was a pleasant morning when the train drew out of Euston at 10 o'clock. When I am going a journey by train, I always endeavour to travel by day. Night journeys are for those who do not wish to waste time or to whom time is precious. Time means nothing to me—except in the matter of a promised appointment—and I should say that this is the greatest boon that moneyed independence brings with it. Not to have to rush here and there; not to have to be at a certain place at a precise time lest one's income suffers—can a man ask for more? But, there I go, like my famous ancestor, moralising before I have really begun.

My chief reason for day travel is that I like to look out of the window at the passing scene. I buy papers and books at the bookstalls in stations, knowing full well that the papers will be merely glanced at, and the books left unread, for I shall spend my day with my eyes glued to the window. For, having sampled almost all modes of travel by land, sea, and air, I am still convinced that one gets a better idea of a country from the window of a railway train than in any other way. Again, there is always the chance of meeting an interesting companion.

In this respect, I was indeed fortunate on my journey to Glasgow. The only other occupant of the compartment was a Glasgow man who, on hearing that I was on my way to his city for the first time, became most enthusiastic about it, and told me many things that convinced me that I was doing a wise thing by going to Glasgow. Naturally, I allowed for a little exaggeration—for what man does not over-praise the city of his birth?—but as my fellow-traveller was a man of some knowledge and culture, I knew that I was going to no uncivilized city peopled by barbarians.

'Then, from what you tell me,' I said, after he had spoken for some time, 'Glasgow is a perfect city.'

He thought for a moment. 'Well, I wouldn't go quite as far as that,' he replied, 'but it's almost perfect. There's just one thing—we get an awful lot of rain. Mind you, it's not only in Glasgow, it's all over the West of Scotland. If it wasn't for the rain I'd say that Glasgow was hard to beat. And talking about rain, I've crossed the Border many times, and I've seen it dry on the English side and raining in Scotland. Not that it's always like that, but I've seen it. Maybe it'll be like that today.'

I confess I was slightly incredulous about this, although I did not say so, but when we crossed the Border I discovered that he was right. I have since learned that this does not always happen, so I was really lucky to see it.

I do not intend to describe the journey to Glasgow, for it was uneventful, but there is one incident that I must put on record. When the luncheon hour arrived, my fellow-traveller insisted that I be his guest. Several times he had spoken of the hospitality of the Scot, and I could see that he wished me to realise that it was no idle boast. I do not as a rule accept offers of meals from strangers, but I felt that his invitation was sincerely meant, and that he would be hurt if I refused, so I accepted. It was my introduction to a hospitality that I was to find embarrassing at times, for in my travels I was to experience none greater in any country.

So much for the journey. We arrived in the Central Station at Glasgow shortly before six o'clock in the evening. A Scots writer once said that to travel hopefully is better than to arrive, but I do not agree. I travel hopefully always, but arriving always gives me the keenest sense of pleasure. I may be disappointed a few minutes later—by the place itself, by the people I see, by my lodgings—but the actual moment of arrival has never failed to give me a particular thrill of pleasure that I hope I shall never lose.

As the train was drawing in to the station, my friend gave me his card—or I should say, his cards, for one was his business address and the other his residence—and a cordial invitation to visit him. 'I hope you'll find our city all I say it is, Mr. Gulliver,' he said, as he looked at my card, 'and if you will honour me with a visit, I shall be delighted to see you. I'm not going to offer to show you round, for I know that you wish to see things for yourself; but if I can be of any assistance to you, give me a ring, my telephone numbers are on the cards. And do come to see me, for I'll look forward to hearing your impressions.' With that he shook me warmly by the hand, and stepped from the now stationary train, crossing the platform to a waiting motorcar. I had decided that I would pay him a visit before I left Glasgow.

So this is Glasgow!

My first surprise in Glasgow was the Central Station. I had not expected to see such a huge building. I do not suggest for a moment that it compares with some of the railway stations I have seen in America or in some of the Continental cities, but it is certainly one of the finest I have seen in Britain. My second surprise was the station hotel, although in a way the size of the station had somewhat prepared me. Yet this vast building, with its long corridors, its spacious lounge which I glimpsed in passing, and its general air of comfort, immediately brought to my mind the remarks of my fellow-clubmen in London about the uncivilized country and the barbarians who inhabit it. And I wished that they had been with me.

After a bath and an excellent meal, I stood at a window of the lounge, watching the shifting scene in the station. But soon I realized that I must become part of that scene, for I cannot resist stations. Nowhere does one see so many aspects of life. I can stand in a busy railway station for hours, literally—I have done it—mingling with my fellows, watching the various types and listening to their scraps of conversation as they pass. Many people would call it a waste of time. I find it fascinating, just as I find it fascinating to sit at a window in the city and watch the crowds hurrying past. This night I had no desire to see any other part of Glasgow.

One of the first things I discovered in the Central Station was evidence that the Scots are not superstitious. There are thirteen platforms in the main station! No one worries about that. I stood at the barrier watching people go on to Platform 13 and not one gave it a thought. Yet I have known places where that number is carefully avoided, although if a thing is the thirteenth of its kind, I cannot see what difference can be made by calling it 12A. But, then, I'm not superstitious.

The station, as a whole, fully bore out my first impression of it. So high and spacious is it that even at its busiest it never seems unduly crowded. It has none of the gloom of so many stations, for the atmosphere is one of brightness and cheer. The same cannot be said of the other principal stations in Glasgow, which I saw some time later. St. Enoch Station looks impressive from the outside, but its gloomy interior is somewhat overpowering. Buchanan Street Station is, well, just a station; while Queen Street Station is so dismal and depressing that even I could not bear to linger in it. Only men with an extra reserve of cheerfulness should be asked to work in Queen Street Station, for only they could bear it.

But I am not concerned with other stations. They may have their points. Regular users may love them. Black as they are, to some they may be comely. I write merely as an impartial observer, and to me none of them compares with the Central.

How many stations are there in this country where you can buy a loaf of bread? I do not know of any other than Glasgow Central. For there is a baker's shop here—not merely a stall, but a real shop, where you can buy anything that a baker sells. I should not be surprised that if you wanted a wedding cake you could get it here. And next door to it is a chemist's shop where you may leave your prescription on your way to business and collect your pills or powders on your way home in the evening. Glasgow has also a passion for milk. One of the busiest places in this station is the Milk Bar. I stood for a long time watching all sorts and conditions of men and women, standing at the bar, sucking milk through straws. I confess that the sight gave me the idea of sampling something stronger, and I made for the refreshment bar. There, however, I did not see the same enthusiasm for stronger liquids that I had seen at the Milk Bar. It may, of course, have been an off night, but subsequent milk drinking that I've seen in Glasgow makes me think that Glasgow really likes milk.

I had wandered about the station for the best part of two hours. Everything I had seen pleased me. The station itself had an air of well-being, the people I saw seemed prosperous and happy, and although I heard much talk and many snatches of conversation, I'm afraid that I could not understand a great deal of it. I have no doubt I shall soon become used to this unfamiliar northern speech, I thought to myself, as I made my way through the swing doors into the hotel, and to bed.

Just as I was dropping off to sleep the thought came to me that I had seen no one wearing a kilt, nor had I heard the bagpipes. Could I really be in Scotland?

Chapter III

I have now been in Glasgow for several days, and I like it. That may seem a bald statement, but my reactions to cities have always been based on first and early impressions. I have found this wherever I go. I cannot give reasons for these likes and dislikes, except that one city is friendly and another is not. I dislike Budapest and love Vienna, although both cities are usually considered to have much in common. Budapest depresses me, Vienna, even post-war Vienna, makes me happy, and it is a friendly city. I never return to Vienna without experiencing the feeling that I have come home. Paris, in a lesser degree, is like Vienna; so is Stockholm; and I found this atmosphere strong in Kuopio, a little city in the heart of Finland. New York—but why go on making comparisons? The thing is entirely personal. A city is either friendly or it is not, and I find Glasgow entirely friendly, although I know no one, other than hotel servants and officials.

But everywhere I find kindness and trust. I

go into cafés—although Glasgow calls them tea-rooms—and I find the tables laden with cakes, muffins, and other eatables. A waitress brings me a cup of tea or coffee; I eat what I want and when I am leaving I tell her what I have had, and she takes my word for it! Nowhere in the world have I seen such trust displayed in a stranger. It at once establishes a feeling of friendliness. I shall have more to say about these tea-rooms later.

And in what other city could this have happened? I wished to change a five-pound note, so I went into a tobacconist's shop and asked for cigarettes, proffering the note in payment. 'I'm sorry, sir,' said the assistant, 'but I'm afraid I can't change that at the moment. You can pay me when you're passing this way tomorrow.' And he had not seen me before! Can you wonder that I find Glasgow a friendly city?

It has never been my practice to rush off to the show places when I visit a city. I take these in as they come, preferring first of all to get the feel of the city. I wander about at all times, except early in the morning, for early morning is no time to be abroad in a city unless of necessity. Thus I have now seen Glasgow at all other times of the day, and despite the remark of my fellow-traveller regarding Glasgow's rain, I have been lucky enough until now to have had nothing but fine weather.

I find it pleasant to wander about in the forenoons looking into shop windows, for the forenoon is the ideal time for this diversion. There are fewer people about, and those that are have business to attend to, and are too much intent on going to it or coming from it to dally before shop windows. Then in the afternoons how pleasant it is to stroll leisurely in the principal streets, thronged with well-dressed people. Women predominate then, and I may as well say it now as later—I find Glasgow women good-looking, well-dressed, and, most important of all, happy-looking.

The Scot is generally referred to as being dour. It has become a convention among writers to describe him as 'dour' and 'raw-boned'. Perhaps outside of Glasgow Scots have these characteristics, but I doubt it. The same novelists refer to the 'strong silent Englishmen'. Most of the strong Englishmen I know are far from silent. These things are legends.

But it is in the evening, I think, that one sees Glasgow at its best. Walk out of the Central Station by the Union Street exit, shortly after

5 o'clock, and one is in the thick of it. Glasgow is going home for tea. Perhaps I should explain here that tea in Glasgow is not tea as other people know it. Tea is a meal that may consist of fish, or ham and eggs, or some meat dish. It is known as high-tea. Dinner is eaten in the middle of the day, and while a small minority eats dinner at night, and has lunch as the mid-day meal, high-tea is the rule with the majority. And very good it is, although Brillat-Savarin would not have approved.

But Glasgow has not yet reached home. It is crowding on to tramcars and buses. There is no give and take here; it is a case of every man for himself, and every woman for herself. One thing and one thing only matters—get on to the bus or tram, even if you tread on the toes of others, and your elbow meets a chin. Tram follows tram, and bus follows bus until there is an unbroken line of each, and still the struggle continues. At less busy parts of the city, queues are formed, but here, that would be impossible.

How good-natured and efficient the conductors are! In the most trying circumstances they never seem to lose their heads or their tempers. They know that their vehicles must not become overcrowded. They know that everybody knows of this and is determined to ignore it at the rush hours. But a quiet, 'Sorry, full up' quells the savage beast.

I take off my hat to the conductors!

For some reason that I cannot fathom Glasgow seems to be extraordinarily proud of its tramway system. Men will listen to almost any aspect of the city being criticised, and will argue the merits of this thing or that in even tones. But speak lightly of the tramway system; suggest that it is just possible that there might be another city in the world that has a better one, and dangerous gleams come into eyes, faces grow angrily red, and the storm breaks.

My own opinion of Glasgow's tramways is that—but, no, I am a stranger within the gates; I have been treated with kindness and consideration. Let me emulate the visiting film stars, but with a slight difference. Let me say, 'I think your tramways are wonderful!'

And now the worst of the evening rush is past, or seems to be. I stroll slowly up Renfield Street in a blaze of ruddy lights. I have only to half-close my eyes to imagine myself in Piccadilly Circus. I have heard people speak scathingly of the illuminated sign. It is blatant and vulgar, they say. I must have a blatant and vulgar

streak in me somewhere, for I like this pleasant
ruddiness. It adds to the friendliness of the atmosphere.

I walk as far as Charing Cross, then turn and
retrace my steps. Already there is a small queue
at one of the cinemas—a tremendously popular
film is showing—and I marvel at the determination of the entertainment-seeker in Glasgow. I
commented on it to the manager of one of the
cinemas that I visited, and he told me that he
has seen a queue standing while snow fell. As
the people were admitted to the cinema, attendants brushed the snow off them.

As I pass down Renfield Street again, the
solitary book-barrow that had carried on after
the others were gone was being covered with its
tarpaulin. At almost every corner in Renfield
Street you will find a book-barrow, and in my
few days' residence in the city I have already
had two 'finds'. One is a first edition of that
classic, *Irene Iddesleigh*, by Amanda Ros, the book
that drew a famous review from Barry Pain. I
could hardly believe my eyes when I saw this
book—for which I have been searching for a
long time—among the 'threepennies'. My heart
almost missed a beat as another man put out
his hand in its direction, but his choice was the

next volume—a book on plumbing. I clutched my *Irene Iddesleigh*, paid my threepence, and went into a tea-room to look at my prize. It was a first edition all right; what was more, its owners had pasted inside the Barry Pain review, of which I had often heard, but had not seen. But that was not all. On the fly-leaf were a few pencilled lines by a reader, saying how much he had enjoyed this book, and that reader was the late Fred Terry, who had autographed this copy, as had also his wife, Julia Neilson.

My other 'find', a few days earlier, was a one volume edition of George Otto Trevelyan's *Life and Letters of Lord Macaulay*. Not a very exciting 'find' you may say—until I tell you that there is a long inscription on the fly-leaf, written and signed by George Otto Trevelyan himself!

I could not fail to have anything but kindly feelings towards a city that could give me two such pleasant 'finds'. Yet, I listen to others turning over the books on the barrows, and as often as not I hear them remark that 'there's nothing but rubbish here'. But one man's junk is another man's joy!

Forgive me for wandering into a bookish by-way. Blame the vendor for being still at his stance when his fellow-vendors had long departed for home. After all, why shouldn't I tell you of my good fortune? You may have the same one day, when all I can see is the 'rubbish'.

My walk has made me happy. I return to my hotel and my dinner. Which reminds me I have been studying the eating habits of Glasgow, and find them most interesting. These will require a separate chapter.

Chapter IV

I t is possible to eat as expensively in Glasgow as it is in London!

It is also possible to get a really satisfying meal for less than a shilling.

I am not concerned here with expensive eating—not because it does not interest me, but because it is not characteristic of the bulk of Glasgow's citizens.

Food interests everybody, for everybody must eat, although some eat merely to keep alive. If you wish to sample such unusual things as bird's nest soup, frogs, snails, and sharks' fins, you may do so in Glasgow. If you would have a curry, as the man from the East knows it, there is a place where it may be had. Does your soul crave a pig's hough, almost overpowering in its size? One restaurant specialises in it.

Those and many other things I have discovered in Glasgow.

While many restaurants are famed for their cooking generally—and there are few places in Glasgow that will not provide an excellent meal

22

at a reasonable cost—others are famed for a particular dish. One I have discovered provides a steak and kidney pudding that Lucullus might have grown lyrical over. Another supplies a jam roly that is so famous that 12 yards of it are cooked every day.

Earlier in this little book I mentioned the high-tea. It is a meal that has been, and is, sneered at by those who know it not. Your Gourmet goes white and shudders when he hears it mentioned, yet to the Glasgow man it is something to be treated seriously.

In this connection I recall an incident that happened in Vienna, an incident the significance of which I did not appreciate, for I knew nothing of Scotland then. I had dined with a Scotsman on the terrace of one of the beautiful hotels on Cobenzl hill. The meal was perfect, the surroundings equally fine. As we lingered over our coffee, I remarked on the perfect meal we had just eaten. 'Yes,' agreed my Scots friend, 'it was indeed fine—but I'd give it all for a Glasgow high-tea at this moment.' And he meant it.

High-tea in a Glasgow restaurant, I find, consists usually of two courses, and the favourite combination is fish and ham and eggs, with sausage and egg as a close second favourite. Toast and butter, with jam, or 'preserves' as they call jam in Glasgow, is an accompaniment, and the whole is washed down with a pot of tea. And how good it all is. It may be that porridge and broth have been responsible in the past for making the Scot what he is, but I think the high-tea has also played an important part in fashioning the Glasgow man mentally and physically.

But I am not so much concerned with what Glasgow eats as I am with how Glasgow eats. I have commented on the tea-rooms, where stacks of cakes, scones, cookies, biscuits, and other delectable things are found in a bewildering array. It is no exaggeration to say that these tea-rooms are full practically all day. Glasgow has a passion for tea- and coffee-drinking. As early as nine o'clock in the morning certain popular coffee-rooms are full of young men who had dropped in for a morning cup before going to the office. I could not believe this, until one morning I investigated for myself and found it to be so.

Then, again, about eleven o'clock, there is more coffee-drinking, members of office staffs going out in relays. Although officially frowned

on in some offices, it is an unwritten law in most
that there shall be a coffee period in the forenoon. Your real coffee hound has another cup
after lunch, and perhaps one in the middle of
the afternoon, and probably one, or a cup of
tea, before going home in the evening. Innumerable deals are brought off over a coffee,
and the actual amount of the liquid drunk in
Glasgow in a year would probably float the
entire British Navy. Or so it seems to me.

Another interesting aspect of the coffee habit
in Glasgow is the number of tobacconists' shops
that have a coffee-room attached. The combination is ideal, and it is a combination that I
have not seen elsewhere.

Several times in the course of my visits to
these coffee-rooms I had heard a mysterious
personage mentioned—one Tommy Dodd. I
began to speculate on the appearance of this
gentleman, and his exact significance, but without arriving anywhere. I thought of asking some
of the people I heard mention his name, but it
seemed like inquisitiveness. I did ask one
waitress if she knew a Mr. Tommy Dodd, and
she thought for a moment before replying: 'No,
he disna come here.'

Then one day all was made clear to me.

Tommy Dodd was not a person, but a method of deciding how the coffees shall be paid for. I was lucky enough to sit at a table with several young men. They had been there for some time, when one looked at the clock and said: 'Time we were moving boys. Let's have a Tommy Dodd.' I at once became interested. *A* Tommy Dodd! The speaker took a newspaper, and marked, with a pencil, a letter in a word. Then the man immediately on his left said a letter—any letter—and the man next to him gave the next consecutive letter in the alphabet. So it went round the five or six coffee-drinkers, until one of them mentioned the letter marked in the paper, provided that a complete round had just been made. The winner received fourpence from each of the others, although actually the cup of coffee costs threepence. If there is a large company this means that the winner of the Tommy Dodd gets his coffee free, plus a few coppers extra.

Although I have made many enquiries, I cannot discover the original of the name Tommy Dodd, not even from those who use it daily.

Perhaps the most interesting of all ways of eating in Glasgow is the quick-lunch restaurant. One is run on American lines. You lift a tray with the appropriate knives, forks and spoons, and make a choice from numerous cold or hot dishes. You then go to a desk where a girl glances at your tray and gives you a bill for the food that you have chosen. You then proceed to a table, unload your tray, and eat.

There are several other quick-lunch places on older lines. One in particular has interested me. It is near the Stock Exchange and is much frequented by stockbrokers and other business men. It is popular also with newspaper men and members of the theatrical profession, several of whom were pointed out to me by a man with whom I got into conversation.

This is truly an amazing place. Go in at one o'clock or shortly afterwards, and you find a seething mass of men, most of them bowler-hatted. Through this munching mass, for many are eating sandwiches, you will see several figures making their way to a corner, holding aloft a plate of mince, so that they can eat it without being jostled. To the onlooker, it is eating in the most uncomfortable circumstances, yet nobody thinks so. To eat here is a daily adventure.

Innumerable plates heaped with every conceivable kind of sandwich occupy a long centre table. At one side of the long room is a bar, at the other a hot plate, where various hot dishes and soup may be had. To negotiate a plate of soup through that lunch-time mob must require years of practice. Even to carry a glass of milk is difficult, as I know, for the first glass I filled was jolted out of my hand by a man who raised his elbow unexpectedly, and most of the milk went over him. He did not seem to be unduly worried, and I decided that it wasn't the first time he had had a milk drenching. We became quite friendly afterwards.

The amount of milk drunk in this place is surprising. The most unlikely-looking men drink it, and I should say that there is much more milk drunk than any other liquid.

Apart from the sandwiches which disappear like snow before a hot sun, the supplies having to be constantly renewed, the two favourite dishes appear to be mutton pies and toasted cheese on bread. The latter is famous, and deserves to be. I have tasted nothing quite like it anywhere. Many men, too, have a passion for cold hard-boiled eggs, and it is not uncommon to see a bowler-hatted man with a naked boiled egg in one hand, and a piece of buttered bread or a cheese sandwich in the other. The sight of this made me lyrical, and I thought out a poem one day as I watched the eaters. Alas, all I can remember are the lines:

> *Where hard-boiled men*
> *In hard-felt hats*
> *Eat hard-boiled eggs*
> *And cheese.*

But the big thrill in this help-yourself restaurant is that you can also help yourself to beer! It may seem incredible, but it is true. You select a tankard, turn on a tap, and draw your pint or half-pint as the case may be. The stranger can hardly believe it, even when he sees it done.

And what about payment? Well, everything is clearly priced; you remember what you've had, and you tell the lady at the cash desk near the door what you owe, and she believes you. That is the crowning touch of the meal. It is a jealously-guarded privilege this, a privilege seldom abused. To the average *habitué*, the thought of understating the amount due is unthinkable. The fact that he is trusted adds to the pleasure of his meal. On odd occasions, some poor, misguided fellow has paid for much less than what he has consumed. He does not

29

'get away with it' for long, *because another custo-mer usually reports him!*

Such a thing is rare. Glasgow is an honest city.

Chapter V

'You must go to a football match,' said a Glasgow man I met in the lounge of the hotel. 'Are you staying over the New Year? You are. Good. Then you must see the Rangers and Celtic match on New Year's Day. It's at Parkhead this year—that's the Celtic's ground. Pity it isn't Ibrox—I prefer Ibrox—but that doesn't matter. You'll have to see that match. You can't leave Glasgow without seeing it. Mind you, it's like no other football match. It is on its own. Look here, I'm going, if you care to come with me. Though I'd better warn you, I'm having only a bobsworth. That means standing —in among the crowd you know—but you'll hear some strange things, and you'll get some fun. What about it?'

I said I'd be delighted to accompany him. From what I had heard, New Year's Day in Glasgow is a rather miserable day, unless you are engaged in a family gathering. Actually, it was much worse than I had anticipated. Every-

body is on holiday, but the day is like the traditional Scots Sabbath. The shops are closed, the
restaurants and tea-rooms, too, and not a
tavern remains open, as the Law says they must
be closed. It must be the most depressing day in
the year for many Glasgow people. I found it
so, and was glad that I had decided to go to the
football match.

We took a bus from George Square shortly
after one o'clock. The Square was swarming
with men, most of them wearing caps, and I
was impressed by the orderly way in which they
queued up to get into the buses that came
along every few seconds. I listened attentively
to the conversations going on around me, both
in the queue and in the bus; they were unin-
telligible. Certain names had only to be mentioned to start fierce arguments. Years of football events were unrolled, and players long
dead or long retired were severely criticised for
shots they missed in matches twenty or thirty
years ago. My friend told me that this sort of
thing was quite usual, but it seemed strange to
me that events so long past should still have the
power to excite men almost to a frenzy. But
then, I am not a football enthusiast, and actually was going to see my first Soccer match in

twenty years or so. Thus the whole thing was new to me.

After passing through a drab district, of which I caught but a glance now and again from the bus window, so intent was I on the remarks of my fellow-travellers, we arrived near the field. A few minutes' walk brought us to a mob controlled by mounted policemen. Gradually the mob was being marshalled into queues by the mounted police, who were by no means gentle in their efforts. But they were effective, and before long I was passing through one of the many narrow entrances to the ground. We climbed some steps, and arrived on top of the terracing, and the field and spectators lay below us.

We eventually took up our position half-way down the terracing and behind the goal net.

It was soon obvious that we were among the Rangers' supporters. Blue was the predominating colour, and innumerable blue handkerchiefs were in evidence, and soon began to wave defiance at the other end of the field, where green handkerchiefs were soon answering. From which you will gather that blue is the Rangers' colour and green the Celtic. Before long, the ground looked as if it could not hold any more

c   33

spectators, but still they kept crowding in, and soon our particular part of the ground became uncomfortably crowded.

It must have been worse elsewhere, for the ambulance men were kept busy with fainting and fainted spectators.

Then somebody started throwing an orange into the air, and, before long, the air was full of tossed oranges. The reason for this I was not able to discover. It seemed an aimless pastime.

I gathered, also, that the one thing essential to the well-being of football spectators is chewing-gum. All around me men were chewing. There was not a steady face to be seen, and in the end I, too, became a gum-chewer. No doubt it helps the vocal efforts of the crowd when the match begins.

I found myself beside some young men from a neighbouring town. Before long I knew all about their private lives, as well as the history of each player soon to come on to the field. All had bottles of whisky and beer which they sampled at intervals. They were good-humoured fellows, particularly one named Jake who was the life and soul of the party. His particular friend stood just at my back, with his face much too near my ear as I was soon to learn. It was not long before Jake informed us that 'the big So-and-So wi' his teeth in his pocket is gonna merry ma sister'. After which he took a long pull at a bottle, then looked at his prospective brother-in-law and said: 'Mac, fur Goad's sake pit yir teeth in. If Aggie seen ye noo she widna hiv ye.'

But Mac's thoughts were far from Aggie at that moment, for the teams were coming out, and I thought that my right ear-drum had burst when he roared his approval of a certain player, much to the disgust of Jake.

By this time the excitement was beginning to have its effect on Mac. He screamed advice to players who had not yet taken up their positions. He made strange noises in his throat, and his language would have made me blush if I were still capable of blushing. Never, at any time or in any place, have I heard so much bad language, and, what is more, bad language used so senselessly. There was a total disregard of syntax. Adjectival swear words were used as nouns, and perfectly harmless words were split up to allow a swear word to be injected. I came to the conclusion that the swearers were not aware of their language, and that actually it meant nothing. But it was crude.

The game had begun, and so had Mac. One of his favourites was on the ball, and looked like doing something with it. 'Aw, look at that boy, look at him. Did y'ever see the like. That's the wee boy tae pit the ba' in the net.'

It was too much for Jake. 'Shut yir face, Mac, an' don't show yir ignorance. Him pit the ba' in the net—he couldna' pit it in his mother's lap!'

'Ah'll bet ye two tae one he'll pit the ba' in the net four times the day,' said Mac, and the bet was taken in shillings.

Then Mac grew vocal again, and advice was shouted to this player and that. He became almost inarticulate when it seemed that the man with the ball was going to do something with it, till he fumbled his kick, and Mac told him, at the top of his voice, that he was 'a something, something big midden,' and where he ought to go to. And so it went on, until Mac's favourite was on the ball again, and this time it looked as if he might really do something. Screams of encouragement came from Mac—then the favourite shot for goal, and shot badly. Mac groaned, and Jake turned a smiling face and gloated. 'That's yir wee boy that's gonna pit the ba' in the net four times the day. Did ye see him. All

36

Ah've got tae say aboot him is that he's hingin' up in every butcher's shop in Glesca.'

'What d'ye mean?' said Mac, puzzled.

'Oh, they ca' them black puddens there,' came the swift reply.

But Mac had no time to reply to that one. He was screaming again, this time at the referee. In vindictive tones he questioned that gentleman's legitimacy, and the legitimacy of his parents and his grand-parents.

And at that moment the crowd swayed, there was an ominous crack, and one of the barriers gave way. My good friend, who had suggested our coming to the match, was lifted off his feet, and thrown against a broken barrier, having his hand badly crushed. While I was sympathising, I, too, was thrown against a barrier post, and I was black and blue for days afterwards. But Jake was unperturbed. He calmly finished his bottle, and as calmly smashed it at his feet. Then turning to the shouting Mac, he again requested him to put in his teeth.

This time Mac replied. 'Nae fear, I kept them in two years ago at this very grun, an' Ah yelled them oot. Ah'm takin' nae chances. They're stayin' in ma pocket.'

Then the crowd began to sway again, and

for the next ten minutes or so I felt sure that gory and mangled pieces of me would be gathered up after the match. It is a horrible feeling to be helpless in a crowd.

'We're clearing out of this at half-time,' said my friend, and I readily agreed. I could not forget that around us on the ground were now several broken bottles, and if the crowd swayed much more . . . Ugh!

Half-time came, and we began to fight our way out. I had not gone far when I found my-self face to face with a very much intoxicated gentleman, who gripped my arm in a vice-like hold, looked at me with glassy eyes, and said 'Hauf a meenit, mate.' I felt sure that he was about to pick a quarrel, for I suddenly realised that I was wearing a blue tie, and his was green, and partisan feeling was running high. I need not have worried. He merely wished to ask a question, and his question was so astounding that I could hardly believe that I was hearing aright. 'Mate,' he said, tightening his grip, and swaying, 'wha' was the name o' the island tha' the great Napoleon was sent to—y'know, after the ba'le o' Wa'erloo? y'know.'

'St. Helena, wasn't it?' I answered.

His face grew grim. 'St. Helena, St. Helena,

tha's place, mate, tha's place. Well, tha's where that —— So-and-So (one of the players) should be sent. See!' And he released my arm and collapsed.

Without further interruptions we fought our way to the top, and eventually got out of the ground. As we left, a man said, 'I paid a bob to get in. I'd pay two to get out if need be.'

'Well, you've seen at least part of a famous event,' my friend said, when we were safely on a bus. 'What do you think of it?'

'Only Jake or Mac could answer that adequately,' I told him.

Still, it made New Year's Day a little less dull.

Chapter VI

For a city so closely bound up with commerce, and the production of ships and engines, Glasgow devotes considerable time and money to the arts. There is a Glasgow school of painting; there is a strong and living interest in the drama; and there is a real love of music.

If you are a cynic, or are content to go by surface appearance, you may doubt that Glasgow is musical. You may draw my attention to the fact that the resident orchestra—the Scottish Orchestra—ends its season with a deficit and a call upon the guarantors. My answer to that is that few artistic ventures ever pay, and the very fact that there are guarantors indicates a love of music that is above money considerations.

I had not been in Glasgow long before I realised that it was a musical city, despite the oft-repeated phrase: 'Of course, Glasgow isn't really musical.' That is said of many cities, and I have usually found it to be otherwise. I discovered that in addition to having its own orchestra, the Scottish, Glasgow had several series of celebrity concerts, chamber-music concerts, annual seasons of opera and ballet, and many amateur societies doing good work. So I went in search of music.

I began by asking a man in the lounge of the hotel if he knew where I could hear some music that night. 'Sure,' he said, 'Harry Roy and his Band are at the Empire. It's twice-nightly.'

When I told him that it was a different kind of music that I wanted, his face changed, and he said: 'Oh, I know. Highbrow stuff. It's St. Andrew's Hall you want. Half a minute. What day's this? Tuesday! You're all right. The Scottish Orchestra's playing to-night. See, here's the programme in the paper. It doesn't mean a thing to me. And there's a fellow with a foreign name going to play a piano con-con-certo, whatever that is. Hope you enjoy it.'

So I paid my first visit to St. Andrew's Hall, and during the next few weeks I saw much of the inside of that place. Glasgow has reason to feel rather proud of St. Andrew's Hall. It is large, dignified, and the acoustics are good, but it suffers from the disadvantages of so many concert halls—it isn't too comfortable. I remarked on this to a man who sat beside me one evening, but he didn't agree. I think he was a regular attender of concerts, and resented any criticism of his hall. His only reply was: 'I find it well enough, and besides I come here for the music.' After which he ignored me completely. Still, I see no reason why concert audiences should not enjoy as much comfort as the patrons of the cinema and the theatre. In the side balconies you sit facing straight across the hall, which means that your head and eyes have to be slewed round to the platform. Both neck and eyes become strained, and I found that I got more enjoyment from a cheap seat at the back of the area. If only the balcony seats could be angled towards the platform! But it seems ungracious to be so critical of a hall in which I spent so many enjoyable hours. And perhaps my neighbour was right, and it is 'well enough'.

I do not intend to give you a detailed list of the concerts I attended and what I heard played, but there are one or two impressions I should like to put down here, impressions not of the actual music played—I am no critic— but of the people that formed the audiences.

A St. Andrew's Hall audience at the Scottish Orchestra's concerts is quite unlike the audience at, say, Queen's Hall, London. There is nothing arty or Bohemian about the Glasgow audience. They are plain, honest citizens, for the most part in ordinary everyday clothes, with a sprinkling of evening clothes, there because they wish to be there, and for one purpose only—to enjoy the music.

I found the atmosphere a friendly one. I liked to get into my seat a quarter of an hour before the concert began to watch the audiences assemble. I soon felt that I was one of them, not merely a stranger in a strange land. But, then, Glasgow is like that. It is a friendly city, and its citizens are so helpful. I have been here but a short time, yet everywhere I go I have experienced the greatest kindness and courtesy. Shop-assistants, tram and bus conductors, railway employees, hotel servants, policemen, casual strangers; all, in fact, with whom I have come in contact, go out of their way to make things easy for me.

It is almost time for the concert to begin. The players have assembled. A burst of applause indicates that the leader has appeared. He is settled in his place, there is a hush of expectancy, then another burst of applause as the conductor appears. There is little time wasted.

The conductor takes in his players at a glance, his baton is raised, and the concert begins.

I find my mind wandering a little, because I am looking forward to the next item, the piano concerto. I have a confession to make, an almost childish one. Ever since I heard my first pianist playing a concerto with the orchestra, it has been the height of my ambition to be such a player. It is, of course, merely a dream, for I am no pianist. I play a little, and that little very badly, but we all have our dreams and this is mine. It is a form of vanity, I have no doubt. I see myself coming on to the platform to thunderous applause. I see myself sitting down at the piano, looking coolly, and just a trifle contemptuously, at the audience; settling myself on the stool, then giving the conductor a nod to indicate that I am ready. Then I visualise myself dominating the audience with the opening descending chords of the Schumann Concerto, and almost hear the whispers, 'This fellow can play!'

You must allow me my little moment of vanity, forgotten completely when the pianist has begun.

The concerto comes to an end, and there is an interval. Half the audience spills into the passages and entrance halls for a smoke, and here one hears how well or how badly the soloist or the orchestra has played.

'My dear,' says a girl, who looks about eighteen, to a youth who cannot be much older, 'you can't have been paying much attention. The cadenza was simply foul.' The young man looks rather sheepish, and mumbles something, and I move on as the lady begins, 'And the slow movement—'

Yet there is, surprisingly, little talk about the music we have just heard. One man is hotly refuting the suggestion made by his companion that the music of Wagner is essentially vulgar, but for the most part the conversations I overhear are about dances, theatres, films, and the chances of this team or that next Saturday. Then I hear someone say: 'Oh, there's X—, you know, the musical critic of the So-and-so.' I follow the direction of a discreetly pointed finger, and see X— holding forth to several other men. I get near to X—, and discover that he is talking about the respective merits of two brands of tobacco.

And so it goes on, until we return to the hall for the second part of the concert.

You find a different type of audience at a Celebrity Concert. For one thing, it is more fashionable. You have the feeling that many people are there to see the performer rather than to hear him. The audience generally is less discriminating. One evening I heard a Very Famous Pianist play a Chopin nocturne badly —that is, for him. His mind seemed to be wandering, so that he struck wrong notes several times. But the applause he won for this was as enthusiastic as the applause given for a really magnificent rendering of another piece.

It was at one of these concerts that I had a delightful experience. The star was a violinist, who included in his programme the famous Bach Chaconne, which, as you may know, is for unaccompanied violin. I must have heard this played dozens of times, and at the risk of being thought a Philistine, it usually bores me. On this particular evening, however, the violinist made it more interesting than usual, and gave, to my way of thinking, an exciting performance. Please bear in mind that I am not an expert, and that the technique of violin-playing is a thing I know little about; therefore, I cannot judge his performance on that score. But the rendering of the Chaconne gave me a thrill that it had never done in the past.

46

At the interval I smoked a cigarette and got into conversation with a stranger. I mentioned how much I had been impressed by the performance of the Chaconne, only to be met with: 'My dear sir, you may know a little about fiddle playing, but you know nothing about Bach. Do you realise that to-night the Chaconne was played in $13\frac{1}{2}$ minutes? Yes, exactly $13\frac{1}{2}$ minutes. I had my watch in my hand, and I timed it! It was dreadful! Joachim never played it in less than 15 minutes! And if Joachim took 15 minutes, no one has any right to play it in $13\frac{1}{2}$. Exciting! It shouldn't be exciting.'

And he left me, snorting.

Still, that concert had its compensations. As I moved away, smarting a little at my dressing-down, I overheard an intense-looking young woman say to a lanky youth: 'I know what you remind me of—has no one ever told you that you're pure Picasso? You are, really.' I did not catch his reply. I'd hate to be told that I was pure Picasso.

I had my moment at the next concert I attended. As I made my way into the entrance hall of the building, an attendant said, 'The band room's down to the left, sir.'

'But why tell me that?' I asked him.

He took another look at me, and said, 'Oh, I beg your pardon, sir; I mistook your umbrella for a violin case.'

And when I come to think of it, I did need a hair-cut, and my hat was dark enough to be taken for a black one.

Chapter VII

A visitor is not long in Glasgow before he is told of two things he must do—see Loch Lomond and have a sail on the Firth of Clyde. Now, while this book is concerned with Glasgow, I feel that Glasgow and the Firth of Clyde—usually referred to, I gather, as the Coast or 'doon the watter'—are so closely bound up with each other that some remarks on that stretch of water may not be out of place here. I had not realised just what the Firth of Clyde meant to Glasgow men, until one evening in the hotel smoking-room, I was drawn into conversation with some jovial fellows who sat near me, and asked me to join them. In the course of our talk, I had mentioned some of the beautiful places I had seen in the world, and as I was holding forth on the wonders of a certain lake in Sweden, one of my companions said: 'Man, have you ever seen the Firth of Clyde? If you haven't, then you've seen nothing. I tell you there's nothing to equal it anywhere. You've the lovely Cowal shore on one side; the

Argyllshire hills rising; the lochs; the—the—' and then he seemed to feel that he was becoming lyrical, for he suddenly put out his hand for his drink, took a long pull, and said, rather shamefacedly, 'Aye, it's great,' a statement which the others confirmed in no uncertain fashion.

So I promised myself that I would visit this place, and although I was assured that I couldn't possibly see it at its best until the summer, I caught the train to Gourock one fine spring morning, for it is from Gourock that most of the steamers ply to the various places on the Firth.

Now, I feel that I ought to warn you here that this chapter is not going to be about the Firth of Clyde. I started out with the best intentions but, as the popular novelists say, 'Fate crossed my path,' and in this instance 'Fate' took the form of a middle-aged couple who threw themselves, panting, into my compartment, the man gasping, 'Gosh, I thocht we were goin' tae lose the train.' Why he thought so I could not understand, for we were not due to leave for ten minutes: but it was not long before I realised that my fellow-travellers were not used to trains. Their journey was actually a novelty for them,

or I should say, for the man, as I learned later
that his wife occasionally travelled in a train.

Let me describe this couple. The man was a
stoutly built fellow, with a healthily tanned face
and a neat moustache. He was cleanly but
roughly dressed in a heavy tweed suit, evidently
his best—'ma Sunday claes', he told me later.
He wore heavy boots, over the tops of which
thick woollen socks slopped. His garb was completed by a raincoat and a cap which he kept
pulling off and putting on at intervals, while he
attempted to light a pipe that seemed to me to
be empty. His wife—he was not long in indicating with a pointing thumb, 'that's the wife'—
sat on the seat opposite, and was dressed completely in black.

They had not been in the compartment two
minutes until I began to suspect that all was
not exactly as it should be with the man. There
was a certain glassiness about his eyes, and his
speech was slightly thick. But surely I must be
mistaken, I thought. After all, it was early in
the day for that sort of thing! Whether or not his
wife read my thoughts I cannot say, but she
volunteered the information that he had 'jist
had a wee drap afore comin' oot. He had a
hang-over frae yisterday, ye see.'

That roused him, and he slid along the seat until he was close beside me. 'She's right, Dad,' he said to me, bringing his hand down heavily on my knee. 'She's dead right. Ah had a hell o' a day yisterday. We wis at a funeral—the wife's mother—eighty-seven she wis, an' a great wumman. Aye, a funeral—an' ye know whit a funeral is, Dad,' and he gave my knee a mighty squeeze. 'So ye see, Ah had a wee hair o' the dug that bit me, and noo we're goin' hame, an' Ah'm dashed gled. Glesca! Goad, whit a place' —all the contempt in the world was in his voice—'jist a damnt rabble, that's whit it is, a damnt rabble!'

At this point, his wife made a mild protest. 'You see, sir, he's no' used to towns, an' then he's had a wee drap.'

'That's right, Dad, that's right,' he continued. 'Gie me the country every time. A man can breathe there. It's mair'n twenty years since Ah wis in Glesca afore, an' it'll be another fifty afore Ah'll go again—an' then it'll no' metter, fur Ah'll be deid then.' And he roared with laughter at this sally, bringing his hand down on my knee with such force that I smarted for the remainder of the journey.

Suddenly he pointed to above my head.

'Whit's that?' he asked, *that* being the lamp that is found in each of the four corners of the newer compartments. 'It's a light,' I said, switching it on for his benefit. His pleasure was childlike, and his astonishment equally so. 'Guidsake!' he said, 'that's great! Man, it must be grand tae be a traveller o' experience. Ah would never have kent that wis a light. My, my, did ye ever!' and for the next few minutes he kept switching it on and off delightedly.

Then the whistle was blown, and the train started. He sat silent for a few minutes, and I thought that he was going to remain quiet. I was sorry, for I was enjoying his talk; but I needn't have worried on that score. After half a dozen attempts to light his pipe, he gave it up, put the pipe down on the seat beside him, threw his cap beside it, and clutched my knee again. 'Dad,' he said, almost as if he were telling me something in confidence, 'Glesca's nae use. It's an awfu' place, wi' its caurs an' its buses an' its rid and green lights an' a' yon croods. A man isna safe.'

'Nae wonder,' said his wife, 'Ah don't know how you're alive the day. D'ye ken this, sir, he paid nae attention tae ony lights or signals, but jist barged across the street as if there wis nae traffic. Ma hert wis in ma mooth a dizen times yisterday.'

'Uch, be quiet, wumman. Whit aboot the stinkin' hole ye took me doon? Fifty feet below the street, Dad; aye, fifty feet. Nae fresh air in yon place.'

'It wis the Subway,' said his wife, 'y'know, the Underground Railway. He's daft.'

'Mebbe Ah am, but ye'll no' get me doon yonder again.' And he chuckled at the recollection. Then he grew confidential again. 'Man, it's fine tae be gaun hame,' said he. 'Ah'll be gled when we're there.' Suddenly he sat up. 'Did you know Doctor Broon?' he asked me. 'Doctor Broon frae Glesca. Him an' me wis great freens, *personal* freens (he laid great stress on the personal aspect of the friendship), an' he widna go shootin' unless Ah wis there. He's deid noo. Aye, he wis the great man. Did ye know 'im?'

I had to confess that I had not known the late Doctor Brown.

'Did ye no'? Man, that's a peety, Dad. Ye missed somethin'. Him 'n me wis great personal freens.'

He became silent for a few moments, obviously letting his thoughts dwell on the

departed doctor. Then, suddenly, his hand
shot out again, came down thud on my knee,
and he said: 'Dad, d'ye think there's gaun tae
be another war?' Before I could answer his
question, he went on: 'Ah hope no'. Ah've had
enough o' war. Ye see, Ah wis a prisoner in the
last yin. Nearly twa years Ah had o' it. Here,
Ah'll let ye into a secret.' He became very confidential, and whispered that this was the first
time he had disclosed his secret. 'It wis like this,'
he said. 'When the War broke oot Ah got fu' yin
day, an' went an' jined-up. When Ah wis sober
Ah wis in the ermy. Mind ye, Ah'm no'
grousin' aboot that, Ah wid a' been in it ony-
wey, but Ah wis fu' when Ah jined.' He laughed
at the recollection. 'Ah liked it fine; it wis a
great life, an' Ah wis lucky. Ah wis on the
Western Front a' the time, in the thick o' it, an'
never got a scratch, no' a scratch. Then Ah wis
captured.'

'Did you have a bad time as a prisoner?' I
asked him.

'Weel, it wisna exactly a holiday. We had tae
work like neegers, an' Ah wis in the saut mines
for a while. It wis the food that stuck me. It
wisna a' bad—the days ye got barley soup wis
great. But when we had tae eat yon soorcraft—

55

uch, weel, Ah jist didna eat it. Goad! Yon wis awfu' stuff!'

'What, sauerkraut?' I said. 'It's not so bad. I've eaten it quite often myself.'

'Wis you a prisoner o' war?' he said, excitedly.

'No, no. But I've eaten it in Germany in peace time.'

He looked astounded. 'Do they mak' ye eat it even then?' he gasped.

I explained that I had eaten it because I liked it. This was too much for him. He roared with laughter, and rolled about on the seat. He drew his wife's attention to me, and described me as 'the queerest yin ah've ever met', and ending with the statement that any man who 'ate soorcraft wi'oot hivin' tae dae it must be daft'.

An admonishing word from his wife stopped his laughter, and he went as far as he could in the matter of an apology for describing me as daft, by saying, 'Uch, weel, it tak's a' kinds tae mak' a world—but Ah couldna' imagine onybody likin' yon stuff.'

Then, for the next half hour, he told me tales of his experiences as a prisoner. They were horrible, so horrible that I cannot write them here. And I am certain they were true, for they were hardly the kind of stories a man would invent, and a man such as he was, in particular. What I liked about him was that never once was he resentful or bitter. He seemed to regard his experiences as a prisoner as being all in the day's work, and although he was in hospital for many months after his release, and had evidently suffered terribly, I never heard him say one harsh word about his captors. Any little kindness he had been shown seemed to remain in his mind. He recalled with great pleasure an episode in Sweden—his batch of prisoners had been sent home via Denmark and Sweden. From his description of the place—he didn't remember its name—I fancy he had been in Gothenburg for a day or two, and he had walked into the country. 'Ah must hiv been an' awfu' lookin' sight,' he said, 'an' a wumman at a cottage door must hiv felt sorry fur me. She waved me in, gied me a big cup o' coffee an' some broon breed, an' although we couldna unnerstaun yin anither, Ah think she kent Ah wis gratefu'.'

'And what are you doing now?' I asked him.

'Ah work on the roads,' he said. 'Ah like it. It's interestin' work, an' Ah'm keen on it—the scientific side o' it. Ah can tak' levels an' a' that, but no' the way a surveyor dis it. Ah dae it in the way they dae it in the Hielans, wi' a couple o' crosses. Ye see, ye fit up yin cross'— and here he began a long and elaborate description of his methods which I could not follow, but an occasional 'yes' at intervals satisfied him.

'That's quite simple, is it no'?' he said, and when I agreed, he went on, 'Gosh, ye should see the surveyor. When he wants tae dae onything he brings oot a thing ca'ed a theology an' keeks through it. Ah've nae time fur a theology. It's a lot o' swank. Ah've telt the surveyor that.'

I have an idea, however, that the surveyor will go on using his theodolite in spite of this.

The train was steaming into Gourock, where we were to join our respective steamers—I had learned, with regret, that we were not travelling any further together. We parted at the pier entrance. As he shook me warmly by the hand, he said: 'Dad, it's been a rale pleasure tae meet ye. Man, if Doctor Broon wis still alive, him an' you an' me could hiv some great times thegither.'

I believe we could, although I don't even know your name. But you're a real man.

Chapter VIII

When I came out of Gourock Station on to the pier, the words of my hotel companion came back to me—'If you haven't seen the Firth of Clyde, then you've seen nothing.' I was not wholly unprepared, for I had been given a foretaste as the train came out of a tunnel half-way from Glasgow—I learned later that it is known as the Bishopton tunnel—and a marvellous expanse of water and hills had burst into view. But I had been too busy with my fellow-traveller to pay much attention to the scenery. Now it was different. I made my way to the steamer, and for the few minutes before she left I drank in one of the loveliest views I have ever seen. The day was fine, hardly a cloud was in the blue sky, and the sun was warm as we lay in the shelter of the pier.

Across the Firth, some miles away, hills piled themselves as far as the eye could see, cut in two places by lochs, which I learned were Loch Long and the Holy Loch. Directly opposite, a village stretched along the shore, and on to the hillside, and a red roof stood out prominently. So good was the visibility that a motor car making its way along the shore road was seen clearly. The village was Kilcreggan. To my right, the Firth was wide, and several big ships lay at anchor in the roads, or Tail-of-the-Bank, as it is called, a name famous throughout the world. In the distance, the smoke could be seen rising from the chimneys of Helensburgh, near the entrance to the Gareloch, and behind Helensburgh was a lovely long sweep of hill, rising to a conical mound. To my left, I could see other villages and a town—Dunoon—and as I stood at the rail, while some seagulls screamed and whirled below me, diving to the water for scraps of food thrown from the galley, I decided that this was one of the fairest places on earth. No doubt, in wet and stormy weather I might think otherwise, yet I am certain that in any weather it has its beauties.

The steamer was about to leave the pier, and I had to see this accomplished. All my life, since I first set foot in a steamer, I have been fascinated by this moment of departure. The gangway is pulled ashore, the telegraph on the bridge clangs, and the paddles or screws begin to revolve. Slowly the mooring ropes slacken, and then comes the great moment when they are slipped off the bollards and cast into the water. I have still a childish delight in this particular action, especially in the splash made by the rope when it falls into the water.

We were off. For the first time I saw Gourock properly. It looked a pleasant place, dominated by a hill, on the top of which was a tower. A great quarry is scooped out of the hill. The town was larger than I suspected when I caught a glimpse of it as I arrived, and I learned later that among its claims to fame is the fact that the first herring ever cured was produced in Gourock in the seventeenth century. That, in itself, was enough to endear it to me, for I have a real fondness for a red herring.

As we left the shores of Gourock, I could not help thinking how lucky people were to live in such a place with so much beauty on their doorstep.

I had decided to go as far as Rothesay, on the island of Bute, a famous watering place on the Clyde. I could have gone further—not in this steamer—but it meant leaving Glasgow much earlier than I cared to leave, and I reluctantly had to postpone a trip through the famous Kyles of Bute. But if I remain in these parts until the summer assuredly I shall see the Kyles. I am told that the round trip to Arran, via the Kyles, on a fine day, is an unforgettable experience.

There were not many people in the steamer at this time of the year, and, for the most part, those that were seemed to be there with a definite purpose—commercial travellers, farmers, and so on. Two middle-aged men, however, had the appearance of being, like myself, out for a day's sail, and when I got into conversation with them later I found this to be correct.

Let me say here that one of the great fallacies in existence is that the Scot is reserved and stand-offish. I have not found him so, either at home or abroad. He does not rush into a conversation with a stranger, nor does he chatter lightly about nothing in particular, but since I came to Scotland I have had no difficulty in entering into conversations with Scots, in trains, smoking-rooms, or in any public places, at any time.

My two middle-aged gentlemen were standing near me, and had got into an argument. One of them turned to me and said: 'Perhaps, sir, you could settle this.' He then began to talk about some former steamer that had sailed the Firth many years ago, but I stopped him. 'I'm sorry, sir,' I said, 'but I am a complete stranger here. This is the first time I have seen the Firth of Clyde or have been in one of your steamers, so I am afraid I cannot settle your argument.'

Although I could not help them, I immediately got the impression that they were glad to meet me, and, lest you think that is vanity on my part, let me hasten to put it right. I do not mean me personally. They were delighted to meet a stranger, someone to whom the Clyde was a closed book, for they knew the Firth intimately, and were bursting to tell any stranger about it. I was not long in discovering that the Clyde and the Clyde steamers meant a great deal to them.

Their names were James and William—their surnames do not matter, although I have their cards, given to me when we parted in the afternoon. James, it was, who had addressed me. They were both business men who had managed to retire early; both resided in Greenock— that town famed for its ships and sugar—and both were in comfortable circumstances. They had been lifelong friends, I gathered, and it was not uncommon for them to take a sail to

Rothesay in the off-season, provided the day was such as we were experiencing.

'We're making for Kirn,' said James, pointing to that little town, 'and then we go on to Dunoon. That's it a little further on—Kirn and Dunoon are almost one—and it's a pity you're not here in the autumn, for you'd see a grand sight—the Cowal Highland Gathering. I tell you, when the hundreds of pipers get together it's a thing to stir the blood.' He turned to the right, and pointed to an opening. 'That's Loch Long,' he said, 'and it's one of the bonniest places in Scotland. Halfway up it divides like a Y and the left branch becomes Loch Goil. You'll have to see these lochs. You can't leave this district without seeing them. There's a point on the road, at a wee village called Whistlefield, away in that direction, where you can see Loch Long, Loch Goil, and the Gareloch, and there's nothing finer in Scotland. Hire a car, sir, and do that Three-lochs trip. You'll never regret it.'

'That's the Holy Loch,' broke in William, pointing to another opening, a shallower one, for we could see the head of it. 'It's reputed to be bottomless, but I rather think that's a fairytale.'

64

James snorted. 'Of course it is,' said he, 'I'm surprised at you, William, even mentioning it.'

We were fast approaching Kirn, and we reached and left that pier without any further conversation. As we neared Dunoon, William pointed to a hill on the other side of the pier. 'That's the Castle Hill,' he said, 'and the statue is of Highland Mary—Burns's Highland Mary.' It gave my two friends great pleasure when I indicated that I knew of Highland Mary, and when I quoted Burns they shook me by the hand. I found that they were both members of Greenock Burns Club, the mother club.

'But you should see this place in the summer,' said James. 'It is one of the favourite holiday places for Glasgow folk, although in recent years many English people have come here too. Sir Harry Lauder used to live here—I'll show you the house as we pass it (he did), but he left some years ago.'

Our next call was at Innellan, a pretty little place which brought forth no comments from my companions; and then we crossed to the other shore to Wemyss Bay. Wemyss Bay, like Gourock, is a railway terminus, and there are regular train services run in connection with the steamers. I could have come from Glasgow to

Wemyss Bay, but I am glad I did not, for I would have missed not only much of the sail but also my pleasant encounter with the 'prisoner-of-war' on my journey to Gourock. Wemyss Bay is an unusual-looking place. It appears to be built entirely of red sandstone. There are many large houses, some of them of the mansion type, a modern castle, and a great ruin on a hill. This, I was told, was once a fine mansion— Kelly House—which was burnt down by militant suffragettes when the agitation was at its height before the War.

From Wemyss Bay, we went direct to Rothesay, first calling at a 'suburban' pier, Craigmore. Rothesay lies sheltered among hills, with a wide bay before it. It is known as the Madeira of Scotland and I can well believe it, for in such a sheltered position it must miss the gales that blow outside. 'Yonder's the entrance to the Kyles,' said James, pointing; 'Man, it's a pity you can't see them,' and there was real regret in his voice. 'However, you'll see Rothesay. We're here about two hours, and we'll be honoured if you'll have lunch with us.'

'This is another great place in the summer,' said William. 'I fancy it's the most popular resort on the Clyde. As you come into the pier there's a row of white-coated porters standing at the edge, pointing at the steamer. They're trying to attract attention and they do it most successfully. I can't imagine Rothesay pier in the summer without its pointing porters.'

'Yes,' laughed James, 'and I can remember that as youngsters we used to point back at them—but they seemed quite used to that.'

We disembarked and made for an hotel where I found that my two friends were well known. We had an excellent lunch, and a short stroll round the delightful town, where the shops seemed to me to be among the best I had seen in a town of its size. I do not propose to say anything more about Rothesay—for it is too well known—but the conversation of my two friends on the journey home was a joy to me. We returned to the piers we had touched, only in the reverse order, except that instead of going back to Gourock we went to Greenock.

We had not long returned to the steamer when I remarked on the comfort and speed of the vessel. 'In all my wanderings,' I said, 'I don't think I have ever seen such fine river steamers or such comfortable ones.'

I found that I could not have said a better thing, for immediately my two friends started to talk on what I was to discover was their pet subject.

'You're right, sir; you're right,' said James, 'the Clyde river steamers *are* the finest in the world. But they're not the same as they used to be. Not by a long way, sir. The steamer we're in just now belongs to the London, Midland and Scottish Railway Company. Before the War, it would have belonged to the Caledonian Steam Packet Company, the steamers run in conjunction with the Caledonian Railway. Those steamers sailed from Gourock pier, and from Princes Pier in Greenock sailed the Glasgow and South-Western Railway Company's steamers. There was keen competition between the two companies, and there was, of course, another competitor, the North British steamers, that sailed from Helensburgh and Craigendoran. Those steamers were affectionately known as "Caley," "G. and S." and "N.B." respectively, and you'd hardly believe how keen was the rivalry, not only among the companies but among their supporters. At school, boys were divided into "Caley" and "G. and S." camps—I'm speaking, of course, of the Greenock-Gourock side of the Firth. I can remember actual fights about the respective merits of the steamers. I can remember another thing (here he glanced slyly at William), a "Caley" boy was willing to respect a "G. and S." boy, and vice-versa, but the boy who supported an "N.B." steamer was considered to be outside the pale.'

'Rot,' said William; 'I was an "N.B." supporter when I first came to Greenock from Helensburgh.'

'Yes, we soon cured you of that,' was James's reply. 'Your head went under the tap quite a few times.'

William laughed at the recollection. 'Well, perhaps you're right,' he said, 'but I didn't become a "G. and S." supporter. I was all for the "Caley" boats.'

James continued the story. 'There used to be a famous race every evening between a "G. and S." and a "Caley" steamer. It was known as the five o'clock race, and the steamers waited at Princes Pier and Gourock respectively for passengers from trains that left Glasgow shortly after four o'clock. Steamers had raced on the Clyde before, but this regular nightly race was different. When the "Caley" steamer put out from Gourock, the "G. and S." would be sighted, and it's difficult to believe to-day the excitement created by that race, and how eagerly the steamers were watched as they made their way across the Firth. Which would get the signal to berth first? It used to be said, jokingly, of course, that in their endeavours to gain a few seconds, the skippers would have the gangways removed while passengers were boarding the steamers. What did it matter if a few passengers fell into the water, as long as the steamer won the race?'

'That's all finished now,' said William, 'and we suffered a great blow after the War. The "Caley" and "G. and S." fleets were amalgamated, and all became L. M. and S. steamers. That was bad enough, but worse was to follow. The new owners actually changed the colours of the hulls and funnels. The "Caley" boats had black hulls, navy yellow funnels and white paddle-boxes. The "G. and S." boats had hulls of French grey, red funnels with black tops, and white paddle-boxes. *And these were changed!* The hulls are black now, all of them, and the funnels yellow with black tops. Man, you'd hardly believe it, but that change nearly broke the hearts of many people in the district, and that's no exaggeration. We're used to it now, but at the time it was a sore blow.'

'Yes, it was that,' said James, shaking his

head. 'It was the sort of thing you might find difficult to understand if you didn't belong to Clydeside. These steamers weren't just steamers —they had personality. To tamper with them was like tampering with the Constitution. But there aren't many of the old fleet left now— most of the steamers are new, so it doesn't matter. Of course, there are other fleets—the Williamson-Buchanan turbine steamers, with the black and white funnels, and the Mac-Brayne steamers, and it's a pity you've been so late in coming to the Clyde, for you've missed a sail on the greatest of them all, the *Columba*. She ended her career two years ago, and she was the bonniest steamer I've seen on the Clyde. Isn't that so, William?' And William agreed.

Then they spoke of other steamers of the past. I can remember but a few names, *Glen Sannox*, *Galatea*, *Madge Wildfire*, *Ivanhoe*, *Talisman*, *Sultana*, *Iona* and *Lord of the Isles*. There were many more, but I have forgotten them. They spoke of the first steamers to sail on the Firth on Sundays, and how, even yet, some people refer to the Sunday steamers as the 'Sunday-breakers.' They talked of skippers dead and gone, and of the way in which this one or that would take a pier, and when I looked up I found that we were almost at Greenock, where I marvelled at the fine esplanade and the beautiful houses on it.

My two friends accompanied me to the train when we disembarked, and they both expressed their pleasure at meeting me, and hoped I would visit them in their homes. I assured them that the pleasure had been chiefly on my side, for they had made my day memorable, and we parted with the kindliest thoughts of each other.

The sea air had made me drowsy, and I slept all the way to St. Enoch Station.

Chapter IX

There are times when I like to do things on an impulse. For no reason whatever, I sometimes board a tramcar or 'bus, hand the conductor some coppers, and travel thus until I have an impulse to get off again. So it was that, one day, on seeing a yellow tramcar marked 'Kirklee,' I decided to go there. But, as far as I am concerned, Kirklee remains undiscovered country.

The tramcar made its way along Sauchiehall Street, past Charing Cross, and then on into new territory for me. We were still in Sauchiehall Street, I noticed, although we had left the shops and were now in a residential quarter. In a little, we approached a handsome red building on the right-hand side, and I leaned forward and asked a man in front of me what it was.

'That,' he said, pointing the stem of his pipe in its direction, 'Oh, that's the Art Galleries, Kelvingrove Art Galleries and Museum. Cost £258,000, it did. I've never been in it myself, but they tell me it's a fine building inside.'

'Are you a Glasgow man?' I asked, after I had thanked him for his information.

'Oh, ay,' he said, 'I've lived in Glasgow all my life.'

I decided to get off and have a look at the Galleries, for I had heard of them, and the wonderful collection of pictures to be seen there. Only a short time before I had read somewhere that in some ways there was no finer municipal collection in the Kingdom. Every school of painting was said to be represented. I knew that Rembrandt's famous 'Man in Armour' was there, and Whistler's 'Carlyle,' and masterpieces by Rubens, Corot, Turner, Raeburn, Millet, Israels, Peter de Wint and many others, and I had heard that there was some very fine sculpture. It was Saturday afternoon, and I thought to myself that perhaps I should have visited the Galleries another day. They were certain to be crowded, I told myself, although I seemed to be the only person making for the entrance.

But then, I was prepared for anything. Only a few minutes before, I had seen some men playing tennis in the open air on a court near the Galleries. Think of it—tennis in February, in the open air in Glasgow! Such a thing seems fantastic, but it's true.

The entrance to the Galleries leads straight into the Hall of Statuary. At first glance, I got the impression that there were many people about, but I was wrong. The statues gave that impression, although there were a few persons here and there, with an occasional one sitting on one of the many park chairs that occupied the centre of the hall.

I might as well confess that I know little about sculpture. Certain statues and groups that move others to ecstasy seem to me simply lumps of cold marble carved into the semblance of human beings. The innumerable nymphs in marble that fill the Galleries of the world might never have been carved for all I care. The countless 'Head of a Girl' or the busts, 'James Soandso, Esq.' leave me cold. I recall the bust of the pious donor of a certain hall to which I was dragged in my boyhood days to hear dreary lectures. The bust stood on a pedestal at the turn of the stairs, and I have been told that the first time I saw it I asked why the gentleman had sponges on his face. The 'sponges' were whiskers, and I never hear the

75

name of this good man without immediately visualising that bust, and its sponge-adorned face.

There are two pieces in the Galleries at Kelvingrove that made a deep impression on me. Both are casts. One is a simple, homely subject, depicting a countryman with a child on his knee. The child, a little girl, is in her nightgown, and is asleep. The little socks and shoes have fallen carelessly to the floor. The man's arms, with their strong hands, hold the child tenderly, and his head is bowed. On his face is stamped all the sadness of the world, and it is almost unnecessary to read the title of this piece—'Motherless.' I do not think I have ever seen anything so poignant in stone. It is impossible to look at this beautiful thing without being moved.

The other piece of statuary is 'A Citizen of Calais,' by Rodin. It is taken from a group and it attracted me immediately I entered. I looked at this noble figure with the striking face and the large, expressive hands, 'long and long.' I found that I wanted to sit and gaze and be still. It satisfied something within me that wanted to be satisfied. I suppose that is the ultimate aim of great art. And, remember, I know nothing about the finer points of sculpture.

I tore myself away, and wandered among the other statues, until I found myself in a natural history museum. Here is a splendid collection of stuffed animals, which always look much less pathetic to me than living animals in cages. Here are giraffes; a full-grown elephant and a young one; a Highland bull; monkeys galore; sea lions and seals; in fact, a complete menagerie of dead animals. I got into conversation with another man in this section, and for ten minutes or so he gave me a most interesting lecture on the teeth of the various animals. I discovered that he was a dental lecturer, and often came to the museum to study teeth. I found that I was completely ignorant about such things. For the first time I learned that the elephant has only eight teeth, and that the walrus uses its tusks to lever itself out of the water on to the ice. When I looked at the huge tooth of an elephant, I could not help thinking what an awful time the animal must have when it has toothache. When I left my dental friend, to whom I shall always be grateful, I thought how full of unexpected things life was. I walked into an art gallery, and before I had been there half an hour, I had learned quite a lot about elephants' teeth.

There is a shipbuilding and engineering section in this museum, and I deliberately avoided it, although I caught a glimpse of it in passing. I had come to see the pictures, and I knew that if I once got amongst the ship models I should remain there for the rest of the day. So, I shut my eyes to the models, and mounted the stairs to the picture galleries.

The first thing I saw was a printed notice, informing me that I could be ejected for whistling or making loud noises. Surely such a notice is unnecessary? Could anyone possibly want to whistle or make a loud noise in such a building? Buildings of this kind always have the opposite effect on me. The massiveness of the building, the height of the roof, make me want to move about on tip-toe, and speak in a whisper. Cathedrals affect me in the same way, and I once felt like this in a Post Office. It was in Dublin, for Dublin Post Office has a cathedral atmosphere.

Only once in my life have I disobeyed a printed injunction in an art gallery or museum, and that was in Beethoven's house in Bonn, which is now a Beethoven museum, containing many relics and manuscripts of the great composer. I found myself alone in a room with Beethoven's piano, on which was a 'Verboten' notice. Visitors were absolutely forbidden to touch the piano. Beside the instrument was one of the many glass cases in which reposed the manuscripts of the master's compositions, and in this particular case, open at the first page, was the manuscript of the Moonlight Sonata. It was too much for me. I simply had to play a few bars of that sonata from the original manuscript on Beethoven's own piano—and I did! I heard footsteps approaching, and hastily I moved into the next room. The footsteps were those of two American tourists, and they had not been in the room more than a few seconds before other footsteps approached. This time it was a caretaker, and the two Americans were given a severe dressing-down for daring to touch the piano. Hadn't they seen that it was forbidden? Despite their denials, the caretaker refused to believe them, and remained in the room until they left. I've had an uncomfortable feeling since that day that I should have confessed to the caretaker and the Americans. If they should happen to read this—which, I admit, is not likely—let me assure them that

I felt rather ashamed of myself. But I *did* play on Beethoven's piano, and from an original score. Nothing can alter that.

I'm afraid I'm wandering away from my subject. After all, this chapter is about the Kelvingrove Art Galleries. In the first gallery that I entered, there were only two other men, both seated before pictures at the other end of the gallery. One had his back to me, the other was sitting side on. He seemed entranced by the picture he gazed at, and I felt I had to see what held him in this way. So I walked slowly and quietly in his direction, but he took no notice of my approach. He was sound asleep!

I walked round to the other man, and found that he was deep in a book. He was so absorbed that I actually managed to look over his shoulder, for I always like to know what a man is reading, particularly when he is held by it. The book was about herbs. Why should a man come to an art gallery to read about herbs? I shall probably never know.

I went in search of the 'Man in Armour.' It is all that has been said of it, and more. I stood for a long time drinking in its beauties; so long that I did not hear another man approach, and was unaware of his presence until he spoke.

'It's a grand thing, that,' he said. 'I come here often to have a look at it. There's one or two pictures in this place that I come often to see on a Saturday afternoon like this. I've known them so long that I sometimes feel that they're mine, if you know what I mean.'

He was a plain, working man by his dress and speech, yet he had the soul of an artist, and we had a most interesting conversation. He deplored the lack of interest shown by his fellow citizens in the Art Galleries. 'Fancy having all this on your own doorstep, and free,' he said, 'yet thousands and thousands of Glasgow people have never been here. I have seen the galleries crowded,' he went on, 'but that was on a wet Sunday. Man, if they just knew what they are missing.'

Perhaps my friend was exaggerating. I merely record what he told me.

I moved on to another gallery, where I found several people, including a group of three men in earnest conversation. As I passed them, I could not help overhearing what one was saying, and it was this, 'So, Ah sez tae him, "Whit d'ye think Ah am? Eh? Any mair o' that frae you, even if ye ur the gaffer, an' ye'll get whit's comin' tae ye, see!" You shoulda' seen his face. It wis—.'

What the gaffer's face was I shall never know, for I passed out of earshot, and went in search of Whistler's 'Carlyle.'

No reproduction of this picture that I have seen has done it justice, to my mind. It is completely and absolutely satisfying—to me, I mean. As I gazed at old Tam sitting there, I can almost swear that his head nodded slowly, and he said, 'Maistly fules, maistly fules.' He was a great man, and his greatness is all here. Whistler knew it. I felt as I stood there looking at the Sage's portrait that there were so many things I should like to ask him, for he had long been one of my heroes. And as I turned away, I felt also that it would have been worth while coming to Glasgow if for nothing else.

I knew I had to leave the gallery then. There was still much to see, and I would come back another day, probably many more days, but I wanted to leave with 'Carlyle,' the 'Man in Armour,' and one other picture, on my mind. That one other is a small picture in a little room. It is an example of the modern Italian school, and is entitled 'Looking at the Carnival.'

The painter is Fosca Fricca, an artist I know nothing about, except that he has painted a picture that has given me intense pleasure. It consists simply of the faces of four men, intent on the Carnival, which is not seen, but you can read the whole story on their faces. It seems a little masterpiece to me.

As I came down the stairs into the Hall of Sculpture, I knew that I would have to see the 'Citizen of Calais' again, and once more I took my fill of it.

I walked out of the building some minutes later, my mind full of this noble work. I stepped on to a tramcar to return to the city, and when the conductor came up for the fares, I handed him a sixpence and said: 'A Citizen of Calais, please.' He looked at me strangely, and in a second I realised my mistake. 'Oh, I'm sorry,' I gasped, 'I mean a penny one.' I felt very foolish. I wonder what that conductor really thought of me?

Chapter X

If you are not interested in the theatre, you can skip this chapter. From time to time I read in the newspapers that the drama is dying, that it is on its last legs, that it is already dead. The cinema has killed it, or is killing it, and if there should be a spark of life left in it after that, the radio is about to finish it off.

The drama has been dying for so many years that people are becoming used to this 'sick man' of the entertainment world, and in Glasgow they refuse to believe that it is even indisposed —for the drama flourishes in Glasgow.

There are nine theatres and music-halls in Glasgow, all going strong as I write; one almost-theatre, if I may call it so, and one small theatre used chiefly for amateur productions.

Before I say anything of the professional theatres in Glasgow, I should like to say a word or two about the amateurs. How many amateur clubs there are I cannot say, but during the early months of the year there is hardly an evening that some little group is not presenting a play. I had some experience of this amateur enthusiasm recently. In one of the coffee rooms which I have got into the habit of frequenting about mid-day, I noticed a group of men, some of them young, and their conversation every day was about the drama. From their talk on production, lighting, staging, and the technical side of the stage, I gathered that they were all enthusiasts. I learned that there was to be a festival at which several clubs were to compete each night for a week, and I decided to go one night. It was one thing to decide to go, but another thing actually to go, for when I went to book a seat, there were very few seats left, and none for the evening most suitable to me. However, I did manage to secure a seat for one evening—the plays were given in a little theatre called the Athenaeum—and I enjoyed myself very much. I am not concerned here with the three plays presented, although the acting and production were much better than I had anticipated, but what did interest me was the audience. The theatre was full of earnest young men and women, many of whom crowded on to a stair outside between the plays to smoke and discuss what they had seen. Their talk, to me, was highly technical—

production and lighting seemed to matter more than the play or the acting—and I gathered that many of them disagreed with the adjudicator's findings the previous evening. As I returned to my seat after the first interval, I began to think that these young men and women were taking it all too seriously, and it was something of a relief at the second interval to hear one man say to another, 'Come on, I think we've time for a quick one.' I thought that was an excellent idea and I followed them to a nearby hostelry, where we got into conversation. They were quite jolly fellows, and they didn't seem to be so dreadfully serious about it all. I discovered afterwards that they were critics, for the newspapers give considerable space to this amateur movement.

Still, I made up my mind after that evening that the drama will never die as long as there are so many enthusiasts in Glasgow. Incidentally, I discovered that everyone in this movement has written, is writing, or is just about to write a play.

Before I leave the amateurs, and deal with the professional theatre, there are two groups that come between, as it were—the Scottish National Players and the Curtain Theatre. The

So this is Glasgow!

Scottish National Players cannot be classed as amateurs, although they are not fully professional. Most of the players belonging to this group have other occupations although some of them spend the summer touring with the company throughout Scotland, taking the drama into remote places. They have presented many original plays, I learned, and I saw an extremely good performance by this company.

The Curtain Theatre also presents original plays, and has a tiny theatre of its own. I saw one of its productions, and again we had work of professional standards. Sometimes this group presents its plays at the Lyric Theatre, a playhouse with an interesting history. At one time it was a regular theatre, the Royalty, owned by a famous firm in the theatrical business. It then became a repertory theatre, and the Glasgow Repertory Theatre, which was brought to an end by the War, is still spoken about with enthusiasm by older playgoers in Glasgow. Then it was taken over by the Y.M.C.A., who still own it.

All this I learned from my coffee-room friends, and it was on their recommendation that I went to see the plays.

When I arrived in Glasgow, and glanced

through the entertainments columns of the newspapers, I decided that this city must be the home of pantomime. Out of the nine theatres and music-halls, seven were presenting pantomimes. Certainly, some were in their last week, but as I write—it is March—four are still running, and one, I am told, will continue until May. This pantomime, at the Princess's Theatre, is unique. It is a peculiarly local affair, which runs longer than any other pantomime in the British Isles. Year after year, practically the same artistes appear in it, and many players famous on the stage to-day have appeared in their younger days in the Princess's pantomime. The subject is never one of the familiar pantomime stories, and the title is usually of the type used this year, 'Tammie Twinkle.' Another interesting thing about the title is that there are always thirteen letters in it. Another feature of this Glasgow institution—for it is undoubtedly that—is that large blocks of seats, sometimes the entire dress circle, are booked by the workers of certain firms who have an annual night out. The theatre is always well booked ahead, and I was fortunate in getting a seat when I did. I shall not attempt to describe the performance. It was four hours of honest laughter. Your high-

brow raves about the Russian players inter-
preting the soul of their country on the stage. I
felt that the players in this pantomime gave us
something of the real Glasgow, or, at least, one
aspect of it.

The pantomime at the Theatre Royal is also
traditional. It was the fiftieth annual production, and this theatre is famed for its spectacular
pantomimes. There is a man in Glasgow—I had
the pleasure of meeting him—who has seen
every one of these fifty pantomimes. This
theatre, I learned, runs its pantomimes for two
or three months, presents several amateur
operatic shows, has a short season of grand
opera, and the rest of the year is occupied by
a repertory company. Even at the height of
summer Glasgow likes to see plays.

The two other leading theatres in Glasgow
are the Alhambra and the King's. Both have
their own characteristics. At the Alhambra,
musical plays are generally to be found. I was
just in time to see a magnificent pantomime
here also. It is a beautiful, spacious theatre,
and the same may be said of the King's,
where straight plays are more favoured. In
passing, I might mention that throughout the
summer both of these theatres run a light en-

tertainment, and I am told they are highly popular.

The newest theatre in Glasgow is the Empire, a palatial building, where first-class Variety programmes are given, although here also a pantomime is run at Christmas. The Pavilion is also a Variety theatre, with pantomime at the festive season, and it occupies a particularly warm corner in the hearts of Glasgow play-goers, I am told. There remain the Metropole and the Empress, both excellent theatres—I sampled them both—where variety and revues are popular. The Metropole has its pantomime, and at one time, I learn, it was the home of 'thick-ear' drama.

I had almost forgotten the Queen's, where I saw a robust pantomime. It has a real old-fashioned atmosphere, with its huge mirrors on each side of the stage. And one has to climb a flight of stairs to reach the auditorium.

This chapter, I confess, reads rather like a catalogue of theatres, but I feel that if I am to take Glasgow as I find it, I must mention those playhouses that play such an important part in the city's life. In the world of the theatre, Glasgow is regarded as one of the most important cities outside of London, and for that reason many new plays have their first production here, before being presented in London.

Come with me to a 'first night.' There is not the same air of excitement here as in London. A 'first night' is not a social occasion—the audience in Glasgow is in the theatre to see the play, and not the 'celebrities' who attend it. There is a fair sprinkling of dress shirts in the stalls, but the majority of the playgoers are in ordinary dress. Unlike a 'first night' in London, there is no moving about in the auditorium; nobody gushes, 'Darling, how wonderful to see you here'; people come in and go to their seats and stay there until the intervals.

The curtain goes up, the play begins, and there is a look on every face that says plainly: 'Go on, let's see what you can do.' When applause breaks out, it is genuine.

As the play proceeds I notice several men who never applaud, and I ask my companion—a Glasgow man—why this is. 'They're critics,' he tells me. 'They never seem to applaud.' I wonder why? I'm sure they must feel at times that they would like to do so.

The first act ends; there is a buzz of conversation as the act is discussed; and quite a few people go in search of refreshment. And, alas,

So this is Glasgow!

quite a few have refreshment brought to them
in the form of tea trays. I say 'alas,' for if I were
a theatre dictator I should forbid tea trays in
the theatre. The first few minutes of the second
act are usually given to the rattle of cups and
saucers. Attention is distracted by a tray being
returned along a row of stalls to a waiting
attendant, and if there is a third act, the same
often happens. Glasgow is not alone in this
form of disturbance, but it is among the worst
offenders.

Another thing I would forbid in Glasgow
theatres if I were dictator is smoking. I am a
smoker, a fairly heavy one, but I see no necessity for smoking in the theatre. At most, an act
of a play rarely lasts more than an hour, and it
is no hardship to ask the heaviest smoker to do
without tobacco for such a short time. Not only
can the smoke be annoying to non-smoking
members in the audience, but it must be equally
annoying to the players. And it is not only the
smoke. One actor I know told me that there is
nothing more distracting to him, when at an
important moment in the play, than the striking
of a match in the auditorium.

But enough of these criticisms. The play is
ending. The curtain falls. The applause is ex-

tremely warm, and I hear a voice say: 'We must have a speech.' And in the end, the leading actor makes a speech. He tells us we are a wonderful audience, and we leave the theatre happy.

As we file out another voice says: 'Yes, pretty good,' which is high praise. For I think of the famous occasion when Mrs. Siddons visited Edinburgh for the first time. She felt that the audience was unresponsive, and exerted all her powers to move them. When she finished her scene, there was a deep silence, then one voice exclaimed, 'That's no' bad.' Then came thunders of applause.

Chapter XI

Glasgow Cathedral stands at the top of High Street. On its one side is the Necropolis, on its other the Royal Infirmary, and opposite it is Provand's Lordship, the oldest house in Glasgow.

That simple statement may seem unnecessary to anyone who knows where the Cathedral is, but I have come to the conclusion that few of Glasgow's citizens know much about their Cathedral, and fewer still have been inside it.

There is an old saying in Scotland, 'The Shoemaker's bairns are always the worst shod.' I have heard this quoted several times since I came to Glasgow—and I expect that there is a certain analogy between this and the fact that Glasgow people have not seen their Cathedral. The shoemaker's bairns are too near to him for their wants to be seen. The Cathedral is too near to Glasgow men and women for its beauties to be realised. You, who read this, may know your Cathedral, and resent my remarks. They are not for you, but for the majority. Let me give you my own experience.

So this is Glasgow!

Several references to a place, Provand's Lordship, had interested me. I liked the unusual name, and when I was sitting in the hotel lounge one evening with two men I had become acquainted with, I asked them what Provand's Lordship was. The first man was frankly ignorant. 'I don't know,' he said. 'I've heard the name often, but it didn't really interest me. I have an idea it's a restaurant.'

'Nonsense,' said the other, 'it's something to do with the Cathedral, I think. Mind you, I can't be certain, for I don't know anything about the Cathedral, I'm rather ashamed to say. Yes, I've lived in Glasgow all my life, and I've never been inside the Cathedral.'

Neither was very helpful, so I had to make other enquiries, and although in the end I did find someone who knew what and where Provand's Lordship was, I had to ask literally dozens of people, Glasgow people, before I obtained the information I wanted. If you are so inclined, ask the next 100 people you meet if they've been in Glasgow Cathedral. If you find ten that have, I shall be surprised. And the same applies to Provand's Lordship, although I should think the number here would be even smaller.

So this is Glasgow!

I set off to discover the Cathedral and Provand's Lordship for myself. I boarded a green tram in St. Vincent Street, and as we skirted George Square and entered George Street, a man in front of me pointed to a building on the left, and said to his companion, 'That's where we pay our income tax.' I should have thought that men would rather pass such a building with averted eyes.

The journey to High Street is short, and soon I was walking up that historic thoroughfare. Two impressions I carried away with me from that short walk, before the Cathedral came into view. In High Street it is possible to have a portion of sausages and chips for 3d. and 4d. I could not help wondering what one got for the extra penny. Was it another sausage or a few more chips? The other thing that I noticed was a book in a window. It was entitled *How to Croon*. Until that moment I had not realised that anyone could want to write a book about crooning; and that anyone should wish to read it seemed even more strange. But perhaps no one does, and it is still in the window, marked down and down until one day it may moulder in the penny box.

Then the Cathedral came into view. I should

say that this beautiful building is seen at its least impressive aspect from High Street. To see the exterior at its best I discovered that one had to view it from the south-eastern corner of the churchyard, for in this way the whole length of the building may be seen. As you enter the gate at the pathway leading to the main entrance, you face the serried rows of tombstones and monuments in the Necropolis, rising on a hill until the skyline is broken by grim pillars, dominated by the John Knox monument. I confess that I found this a somewhat awesome sight. Here was the majesty of death rather than the peace and quiet of it to be found in a country churchyard, or in the flat tombstones in the Cathedral grounds.

I entered the Cathedral and immediately the great beauty of the place enfolded me and brought with it that sense of peace that I always find in such buildings, particularly when I am alone, as I was on this occasion. For a time I had the Nave to myself. There was no incongruity such as I found in Cologne Cathedral, where on a pillar is a notice in three languages, 'Beware of Pickpockets.'

Now, it is not my intention to describe Glasgow Cathedral in detail. For such information you must go to the many books and pamphlets that exist, all of which deal with its history and architecture, and all of them written by much abler pens than mine. I merely wish to record my impressions of this lovely building, so austere and simple in its design and so noble in its atmosphere. I would like to quote from something that was written about it by the Rev. Lauchlan MacLean Watt, D.D., who was Minister of Glasgow there from 1923 till 1934, and is a distinguished Scottish clergyman and writer. He wrote:

The Cathedral has been for practically eight hundred years the Parish Church of the City of Glasgow, and the centre of its history. The rise and development of free urban communities, with the spread of wealth and intelligence, and the decline of feudal and monastic systems, between 1180 and 1240, mark the Cathedral era in Europe. The Scottish period extended from 1165 to 1286, and during that stretch of time Glasgow Cathedral was thrice rebuilt, namely under Jocelin, Walter and William de Bondington (all bishops of Glasgow). It is a monument, not only of these great ecclesiastics, but of forgotten artists and men of genius who carried into their labours the best and most beautiful traditions of their craft, influencing all who came after them.

The rebuildings to which the above writer refers were made necessary by fire. The original Cathedral, or the first one of stone, was dedicated in 1136, and some years later was burned down. The second building was completed in 1197, and of this structure all that is left is a single wall shaft which rests upon a small piece of bench table. The Cathedral Church that exists to-day was begun by Bishop William de Bondington (1233-1258) and during his lifetime the Quire and the Lower Church were completed. The Nave dates from the end of the thirteenth century or the beginning of the fourteenth. To Bishop Cameron (1426-1446) goes credit for a large part of the Sacristy and the completion of the Chapter House, and the last of the builders, Archbishop Blacader (1483-1508) erected the Quire Screen, and added the aisle which is named after him.

But here I am doing exactly what I intended not to do. These few details, which I found in one of the many books I referred to, give you who read this some idea of the Cathedral's age. Its site is on high ground, ground that has been sacred for more than 1500 years, and ground in which Saint Mungo or Kentigern, Glasgow's patron saint, is buried.

I walked slowly round the Nave, looking at the tattered banners on the walls, relics of 'battles long ago'; then into the centre to drink in the beauty of the Quire Screen or Pulpitum, erected by Bishop Blacader at the end of the fifteenth century. It almost divides the church in half, and one of the attendants, who had joined me for a moment, told me that it is the only screen of its kind to be found in a non-monastic pre-Reformation Church in Scotland. A huge curtain towers above it, and I could not help noticing two hot water radiators in the loft of the Screen, which seems a pity, although they are fairly well hidden, but not quite well enough. Incidentally, Glasgow Cathedral is the best heated building of its kind that I have ever been in.

I remarked on the beauty of the building to the attendant. He agreed—then told me that it had just been vacuum cleaned! The only other disturbing note in the Nave was the newness of the chairs.

I passed through a low doorway into the Quire itself, another noble building. At the far end are four chapels dedicated respectively to St. Ninian, St. Martin, St. James the Greater and SS. Stephen and Lawrence. There also will be found *The Reader's Bible*, a black letter volume dated 1617, complete with chain by which it was attached to the Lectern. There is also a preacher's hour-glass, which runs for 38 minutes. They liked their sermons longer in the old days. Some ancient pewter plates and flagons, part of an early Communion set are also to be found here, as well as three metal Communion tokens dated 1725, 1776 and 1819.

Into the Sacristy on the left I went, passing the only original door left in church. It is of oak, and in it are embedded leaden bullets which tell their tale of less peaceful times. The Sacristy itself is a lofty apartment with a centre pillar, on the capital of which are the arms of King James I, and of Bishop Cameron, the builder. The Bishop's Shield is also above the generous fireplace, in which I noticed that a fire was set. This must be a wonderful apartment when a great fire is casting shadows all around.

I retraced my steps and descended to the Lower Church. I called it the Crypt, but was informed by an authority that this is wrong. This Lower Church or Crypt is said to be the finest in Europe, and has been called 'the greatest art treasure of mediaeval Scotland.' I was entirely alone in this dimly lit place, for the afternoon was beginning to draw in, and the small party of Boy Scouts and the two young lovers that I had encountered in the Quire were still there when I left. Faintly, as from a great distance, I heard what seemed to be the sound of an organ, although it may have been the hum of traffic outside. In the centre of this Lower Church is the tomb of St. Mungo, where his shrine once stood. It was too dark to see it properly, for although there is electric lighting the lights were not on.

Through this dim place I walked to the Chapter House, through a beautiful carved doorway, and into the apartment where a great bell stands. It is a sixteenth century bell that did duty until 1896 when it was replaced. Beside it lies the great metal tongue. On one of the walls of the Chapter House is a tombstone that was taken from the churchyard. It belongs to the seventeenth century, and was erected to the memory of nine Covenanters. Inscribed on the stone are the names of the nine men, and a quaint verse, part of which I copied as well as I could in the dim light.

> *Years sixty-six and eighty-four*
> *Did send their souls home into glore,*
> *Whose bodies here interred ly*
> *Them sacrificed to tyranny.*

The two concluding lines of this quaint epitaph consist of a warning to the slayers of the nine Covenanters.

> *They'll know at resurrection day*
> *To murder saints was no sweet play.*

When I had copied these lines, I made my way to the Nave again, which was silent and empty, and as I stepped into the open air, two aeroplanes went roaring overhead. The sound brought me back from the dim past in which I had spent the last hour or so, to the realities of the moment. It was inevitable that I should think how all this beauty and peace I was just leaving could be smashed and destroyed by a few bombs dropped from one of these terribly efficient machines now becoming black specks in the distance. It was a horrible thought, and I shook it off as I approached Provand's Lordship, that stands across the open space beside the Cathedral. This very old house was originally the home of the Master of St. Nicholas Hospital, and was erected in 1471. A three-storey building, it is the only pre-Reformation house standing in the city to-day. Despite its age, the bell on the door is a modern press-button one, which has to be rung, so that the custodian may admit the visitor. The house is now a museum with a lecture room where historical lectures are given regularly.

The rooms contain a wonderful collection of sixteenth and seventeenth century furniture and other articles such as pottery, glass, pictures, Flemish tapestries and some fine examples of sixteenth century stained glass. There is a set of ten William and Mary high-back chairs in walnut that made my mouth water, while the Scottish carved oak arm-chairs, each dated, and many with armorial bearings, form a collection that is said to be without a rival. Lovely as they are, however, I could not help thinking that the early Scots did not go in for comfort as we know it.

When I had paid my sixpence to the custodian, a very pleasant and helpful lady, she told me that I was the first visitor that day. 'But we have many visitors in the course of the year,' she told me, 'and many from abroad, from every part of the world.' I was signing the visitors' book at that moment and noticed signatures from South America, South Africa and Australia in the few pages I turned over.

'What of Glasgow visitors?' I asked.

'Yes, we have quite a few, but very often they come because a stranger has asked to be taken. At the same time, lots of Glasgow people come here, even if lots more have never been, and couldn't tell you where the house was if you asked them. I'm expecting a party of Boy Scouts any minute now.' They were the same Boy Scouts that I had seen in the Cathedral.

The custodian was most helpful. She showed me things I might easily have missed. For example, a delightful little portrait of Mary Queen of Scots, the first portrait I have seen of that much-discussed queen that made her really pretty. Mary is seen in this portrait as a young fresh-complexioned woman. Beside this portrait is one of Darnley. 'It's an interesting picture that,' said the custodian, 'for you'll see that Darnley has black hair, yet according to all accounts his hair was very fair. But come upstairs and I'll show you the room where Mary slept.'

When Queen Mary visited Glasgow in 1566

to see her husband, Lord Darnley, she would not stay in the house where he was lodging then, for he was ill. This house was near at hand, and there is a strong case for her having occupied Provand's Lordship at that time. I was shown her bedroom, with its canopied four-poster, and an oak cradle beside the bed. Elsewhere there were stone window seats, on one of which she is said to have sat and looked out from the window. I sat on it myself, and as I looked across past the Cathedral, the monument of her great enemy was the most striking thing to be seen. But it was not there when the Queen gazed from the window.

From room to room I wandered, looking at the beautiful things they contain, and the interesting relics of a Glasgow that has passed—the old play-bills, ancient bank notes, and such things. As with the Cathedral, a leisurely walk round is no use—one needs days to take it all in. Before I left, the custodian showed me the front of the house, which is now the back. It is a seventeenth-century addition, so that now the front as we see it is fifteenth century and the back seventeenth.

And here I must leave the past and return to the present, promising myself that before I leave

So this is Glasgow!

Glasgow I shall have a full day in Provand's Lordship. I walked down High Street as far as the Tron Steeple. On the pavement, at the base of the steeple, were chalked these words:

'Long live Trotsky and World Revolution.'

Then I looked around me at the men and women in the street going about their business, orderly, soberly and decently, and the absurdity of that inscription in that place made me laugh aloud, much to the surprise of a man who leaned against the steeple.

I saw him watching me as I moved into the stream of pavement traffic, and I'm sure he thought me slightly mad. It doesn't do to laugh out loud if you are alone.

Chapter XII

Coming into the city from an outlying district, I had passed one evening a huge neon sign on the front of a building. The sign depicted a man pushing a barrow, and the place it advertised was Barrowland. I was in a bus at the time, but I made up my mind that I would return later, and see something of Barrowland.

Barrowland is a huge market place in the Gallowgate and London Road district. It consists of a large covered enclosure, beside which stands the Barrowland Palais, a large dance hall, about which more later. In this huge enclosure are innumerable barrows or stalls, where almost everything you can think of is sold, mostly second-hand. In addition, many open spaces in the vicinity are occupied by barrows and stalls.

It is an aspect of Glasgow that many people do not seem to know, and I must admit to finding it most interesting. I have seen open and covered markets in many parts of the world, but none quite like Barrowland.

So this is Glasgow!

I was lucky in meeting a man who knew Barrowland, and he told me something about it as we made our way towards it. 'Saturday and Sunday are the great days,' he said, 'although there is not so much noise outside on Sundays, as "barking" is forbidden. The place is excellently managed and controlled, and is not just a haphazard collection of barrows.'

'But what do they sell?' I asked.

'Practically anything, as you will see. There's a tremendous amount of junk, but no matter how useless it may appear to you, there's always something that somebody wants. But here we are; we'll go into this section first.'

With difficulty we forced our way into a crowd that was thronging a covered market. 'Forced our way' is literally correct, for we had to push to enter, and politeness went by the board. And what a motley collection of people and junk there was. All sorts of men and women were to be found here—well-dressed and ill-dressed, clean and not-so-clean, thin and fat, tall and short, and, as far as I could see, with the exception of ourselves, intent on buying something. The number of Lascar sailors to be seen was surprising to me, surprising when I tell you that they were mostly intent on spring mattresses, which they fingered and pushed and prodded.

'You needn't be surprised at that,' said my companion, 'these fellows are always keen about spring mattresses. I've often seen them carrying one away from here. They buy the most surprising things. Look, there's one with the frame of a bicycle, part of a grate and a bird-cage.'

The particular section we were in was chiefly full of grates of all kinds and sizes, old stoves, iron bedsteads and spring mattresses, workmen's tools, in which a very brisk trade was being done, and several stalls were selling watches and clocks, as well as spare parts. At the same time you could have your watches or clocks repaired. Then I came on a heap of sewing-machines. One, a small hand machine—by its look I should say it was the original one—was priced 1/-. There was a stand where second-hand books were on sale. There was hardly any room to move in it, for the books were not only piled high to the roof but were stacked round and round until they must have been twenty or thirty volumes deep. The stall-holder could not possibly know what he had in his stock, and

even if he did, only an earthquake could have
shifted that solid wall of books.

All the time we were struggling round this
section, music was coming from a gramophone.
A strange feature of this gramophone music
was that almost every record played was an
Irish song. I remarked on this and was told that
it was always so. 'Incidentally,' said my in-
formant, 'these aren't second-hand records,
they're new. And they're very popular. Just
watch how they're selling.' He was right. They
were selling like the proverbial hot cakes.

From gramophone records it was but a step
to wireless sets and spare parts. There was a big
trade being done, particularly in spare parts,
and some of the stuff I saw changing hands appeared to be completely out of date and useless.
Yet every buyer knew what he wanted, for in
this section people were not being importuned,
they were bent on getting something. Outside,
it was different, where the patent medicine
vendors, linoleum merchants and others were
shouting their wares. Just as we were leaving
the enclosure—I felt I wanted some freedom
and fresh air—my eyes were attracted by
two notices, printed in ink on white cards.
They were affixed to a supporting strut by

drawing pins, and were at the stall of a grate merchant.

One ran as follows:

REMEMBER

YOUR EYES YOUR MERCHANT

YOUR MONEY YOUR GUIDE

The other was more to the point, and ran:

A BAD BARGAIN

IS VERY MUCH BETTER THAN

A BAD MARRIAGE

It was something of a relief to get into the open again, and here we saw a different type of vendor. Several men had gathered small crowds while they demonstrated patent darners, while another man was selling a patent needle that could be threaded in a much easier way than the usual type. He was an extraordinary salesman, for he completely ignored the crowd, and simply kept on demonstrating his needles, with his head bent over his busy hands, while he talked in a low voice to himself. Probably he had found that this was a good method, for his wares were selling.

The linoleum sellers seemed to me to have a hard job. Rolls of linoleum are not the lightest things to handle, yet they had the trick of it, and seemed to find it easy. Those lino sellers had a grand brand of patter. If they brought a roll down to its lowest price, and still nobody bought it, the salesman would ask, more in sorrow than in anger, 'Have you no money—no floors?' and that often did the trick. Then another 'smashing bargain' would be unrolled, and as suddenly rolled again, for a policeman was approaching, and it is evidently against the law to have the linoleum spread over the pavement.

Then a deep voice from the next stall tells us that he is 'positively throwing these watches away. Look at them, ladies and gentlemen, look at them. See this one, a ten years English service lever (whatever that means) and only three-and-sixpence.' Then he tells us that he has been in London all week; has arrived back in Glasgow only this morning; speaks contemptuously of London—'What's London! I ask you.' and praises Glasgow and Glasgow people. And he sells his watches.

A racing-tipster is now selling tips, and giving an imposing list of winners that he has provided. We are now coming to the medicine men. One of them is holding a small bottle aloft, while he tells a crowd that appears to be swallowing his every word, and will soon be swallowing his nostrum, that he's not selling it for 5/-. No, not for 2/6, but for 1/3 a bottle. 'Think of it, gentlemen, 1/3. And you shall sample it before you buy.' An assistant then takes round a crystal jug full to the brim with the liquid, and it is well sampled. It was guaranteed to cure anything from gastric ulcers to housemaid's knee.

At another stand, a masseur was telling an enraptured crowd how he had cured cases that had been given up as hopeless. Behind him was an imposing array of printed testimonials, and he had no difficulty in persuading people to come up and be massaged. One young man took off most of his clothes.

I noticed that many of these medicine men quoted liberally from the Bible. That was more than another vendor (not a medical one) did. Between each lot of his goods being offered for sale, he told dirty stories. I found his patter rather embarrassing, and didn't wait there long.

There was a man with a fine crop of hair, and it wasn't surprising to find that he was selling a hair-restorer. He certainly was a good advertisement. Another man, from time to time, flourished a large roll of notes, but why he did so I could not discover, unless it was to show us that there was money to be made at this game.

'There *is* money to be made,' said my companion, when I mentioned this. 'I see one vendor driving up here at times in one of the most expensive cars on the market today.'

For some time I had seen people passing carrying paper bags with holes in them, and I became more and more interested. 'Oh, these! They've bought birds, and are taking them home. It's the easiest and cheapest way. It's the same when you buy a tortoise, only the bag is stronger then.'

And now we had reached a stand where new and second-hand umbrellas (railway unclaimed property) were being sold. There was no raucous shouting here. The whole thing was conducted in a most gentlemanly manner. A well-dressed middle-aged man courteously suggested to a large crowd that it was just possible some of them would like to buy an umbrella. There were stacks of umbrellas, and he selected one. He opened it, extolled its good points, tested its silk, and asked for an offer. No offer was forthcoming, so he suggested 8/- as a price himself. No! 'Well 6/- then! What, is it possible!

Well, well, 5/6—5/-—4/-—3/6—3/-—2/6—2/2 my lowest price 2/2. Come now 2/-. Not a penny lower 2/-.'

It was a lady's umbrella, and not a very large one, yet a very large lady, one of the largest I have seen in Glasgow, could not resist that 2/- offer. She bought the umbrella. I think she got a bargain, although I could not see that small umbrella providing adequate protection for her. Several other umbrellas were disposed of, and then the vendor stepped down from his place, and another stepped up. I was sorry, for I had been fascinated by the way in which the first man rolled his umbrellas. They were no thicker than a walking-stick, and he did it with a minimum of effort.

The newcomer began by telling us something about himself, and the former seller, who was his brother. He also was a well-dressed pleasant man, who was perfectly frank with us. 'You know nothing about umbrellas,' he told us. 'You've bought them, you've used them, but you know almost nothing about them. Now, I do. I've been brought up with umbrellas all my life. I've lived umbrellas. I know the umbrella from A to Z, and if I tell you an umbrella's a good umbrella, you can take it from me that it is. My business is to sell umbrellas. I want to sell as many as I can in as short a time as I can. Now, here's a nice specimen. The silk on that alone would cost you more than 12/- if you were buying it. Mark that—the silk alone, not including the stick or the handle or the frame. But I'm not asking 12/- for the complete article. This is a bargain. Who'll give me 8/- for it. Come 7/-—6/-.'

I had to tear myself away, for I felt that I would end by buying that umbrella that I didn't need. It's a long time since I listened to two such persuasive salesmen, and they worked quietly. I'm sure their quietness pays.

Our next move was into another covered market, where second-hand clothes predominated. What an amazing collection of cast-off clothing was here. The passages between the barrows and stalls were narrow, and the going was slow. Occasionally we were held up while a customer tried a dress against herself. More intimate garments were measured in the same way. A Lascar sailor debated for a long time whether or not to buy a pair of pink corsets. In the end he decided against, although later he seemed to have fallen for a vivid jumper.

Amidst one heap of old clothes, almost

covered by them, sat a small boy absorbed in a book. Even when a garment was pulled from under him to be spread out for a likely buyer, he did not lift his eyes from the book. He seemed to have an indulgent mother.

New caps were being sold for a shilling. There was a wonderful array of them. A scrap of mirror lay on the barrow, and in this you examined the 'set' of the cap—'bunnet' seems to be the correct term here—and when you found a satisfactory one, you paid your shilling and went on your way.

I had had about enough of it by this time but I thought I'd like to have a talk with the manager of this great concern, so I asked a stall-holder where I should find him. 'In there,' he said, pointing over his shoulder with his thumb to a double door. So in we went. The door led into the Palais de Danse of which I spoke earlier. It was closed at that time of the afternoon, and if there is anything more desolate than an empty dance hall, I have yet to see it. We climbed several flights of stairs in silence, and then there came from what seemed a long way off the sound of music. We eventually traced the music to a certain part of the building, and pushing a door open found ourselves in the main dance hall. On the platform sat a solitary saxophonist, practising his instrument. He stopped, and looked at us in a rather startled way. 'We're looking for the manager,' we told him. 'Can you tell us where his office is?'

He could and did, and we went there, but found no manager. We wandered into cloakrooms, kitchens, and ante-rooms, but still no manager. In the end we left without seeing him. Perhaps the saxophonist told him later that two suspicious-looking fellows were in the Palais. If he reads this book, he'll know that we were perfectly innocent searchers after information. One thing I did notice as we came down the staircase. The main chandelier in the staircase roof is in the form of a barrow wheel. A rather neat touch, I thought.

We left Barrowland and walked along the Gallowgate. I'm glad we did, for otherwise I should have missed the tattooer's shop. The window is full of designs for chest, back and arms, 'from one shilling upwards.' For the same price, upwards, unsightly blemishes are also removed. Some of the designs are most elaborate, but the faint blue dot that I wear between the thumb and forefinger of my right hand is all the tattooing I shall ever want. Yet I wouldn't have missed that window for a lot. It seemed the perfect end for such a day as I had had.

But, as the Americans say—was I tired? And as the Americans reply—I'll say I was!

Chapter XIII

In my wanderings around Glasgow, I had been impressed by the number of parks I had seen. No other city that I have visited seemed to have so many parks, and I made a mental note that I must visit them, or at least some of them.

I had thought no more about my visit, until one of the parks came into the news on account of a proposal by some members of the City Council to close it in the evening. This was Kelvingrove Park, and the suggestion that it should be closed in the evening created quite a stir in the Council. In the end it was decided to let it remain open.

The incident, however, turned my thoughts to Glasgow's parks again. There are over twenty of them, and I felt that I could not visit them all. I decided to see six of them. Kelvingrove, on account of its being in the news, had to be one, and I felt that Glasgow Green had to be another: but which four of the others should I see?

So this is Glasgow!

When in doubt, I find the old pin method as good as any. I made out a list of parks, shut my eyes, and jabbed the paper with the pin. It indicated that I was to visit Hogganfield Loch Park, Rouken Glen, Queen's Park and Victoria Park—in addition, of course, to Glasgow Green and Kelvingrove Park.

I decided to visit Glasgow Green first, for it is at once the oldest park in Glasgow and probably the most interesting, being closely bound up with the history of the city. I am glad that I chose Glasgow Green, for it was responsible for my meeting a most helpful and pleasant man, who accompanied me on my other park visits, and gave me much information about them, information that I might not otherwise have acquired, for I hate reading guide books.

Our meeting was one of those casual, accidental things that often lead to a friendship, for I do not think I am overstating the matter when I say that Robert B—— and I are now friends, despite the difference in our circumstances. For Robert B—— is what is known as a working man, and I use that term in its highest and best sense. He is a fine type, an excellent workman in every way, if I am any judge of character, independent in his outlook, well

read—he quoted Carlyle that first day we met—
and with a comprehensive knowledge of the
history of his own city. Yet I don't suppose his
income had ever been more than £3 or a little
more in a week.

You may wonder what he was doing in
Glasgow Green in the forenoon of a fine spring
day. That is easily explained. He was conval-
escing after a severe attack of influenza, I
learned later.

Our meeting, as I have said, was casual.
There were not many people about in the particular part of the park in which I was, and as
he approached slowly, I decided to ask him
something about a building I had noticed.
'That's the People's Palace,' he said, 'it's a
museum and art gallery. You're a stranger here,
sir?"

I admitted that I was, and something about
him prompted me to tell him that I was intend-
ing to take a look at several of Glasgow's parks,
and that I knew absolutely nothing about them.

He smiled pleasantly. 'Well, if I'm not in-
truding,' he said, 'I know a little about some of
them, and this one in particular. I'm just
having a walk round myself if you care to come
with me.'

'I'll be delighted,' I said, and we moved on together.

'Yes, that's the People's Palace,' he went on, 'and that large glass erection beside it is the Winter Garden. There's sometimes music there. It's an interesting place, the museum, particularly if you're keen about old Glasgow, and there's some fine pictures and statues in the galleries. In the museum you'll find a collection of old Volunteer uniforms and other things connected with the Army. You see, the Green has a military history, as it were. Bonnie Prince Charlie's army camped here, and many a time in the days when Napoleon was a menace, the Volunteers used to gather here. They used to have military displays here, too, in my father's time, and I've a faint recollection of seeing one myself. Talking about Prince Charlie, in the '45 affair, a Highland soldier who went over to the Jacobites was publicly executed not far from here. He was shot. In the old days, soldiers were drummed out and flogged in public too.'

'I suppose the Green has been a public park for a very long time,' I said.

'Well, I'm not very good at dates, but it's been looked after by the Town Council since about the middle of the seventeenth century. It must have been a wild place in those early days. I've read that it wasn't safe at night, for highwaymen and other gentlemen of the kind were on the prowl. It was the accepted thing then for butchers to dump their offal at one part of the Green—there was a pit for such refuse—and cock-fights were held on the Green also. And there was a bleaching green which is still in existence.'

'And what is that?' I said, pointing.

'Oh, that's the Nelson Monument. I've read somewhere that an authority has said that it's the finest piece of statuary in Glasgow.'

As we walked round, my guide showed me many interesting things. There was an archway, a grand piece of work which is known as the McLennan Arch. It was the entrance to a famous Glasgow building, the Old Athenaeum, and was designed by Robert Adam. Then he pointed out a fountain which he called the Hugh Macdonald Fountain, which had originally stood on Gleniffer Braes, 'they're in Paisley,' he went on, 'Tannahill you know.' (I didn't then, but I do now.) There was something vaguely familiar about the name Hugh Macdonald, and when I asked about him and learned that he had been a writer, I knew why the name was familiar. Only a few days before, I had picked up on one of the barrows for 6d., a little volume entitled *Rambles Round Glasgow*, by Hugh Macdonald, which I had promised myself to read at some future date.

Another fountain he pointed out is the Doulton Fountain. 'That was a big attraction at a former Glasgow Exhibition. It was held in 1888 in Kelvingrove Park, where the two others since then have been held, in 1901 and 1911. It'll seem strange to have an Exhibition in another park this year.'

In the course of our walk he drew my attention to an open-air pulpit, an open-air gymnasium, and told me that there were over 20 football pitches, 10 tennis courts, 6 bowling greens and several other facts, for he certainly knew his Glasgow Green.

'And this,' I said, pointing to the river, 'is this the Kelvin?'

That made him smile.

'No,' he said, 'it's a much greater river—the Clyde. You should see it later in the year when the small boats are out. Rowing is a favourite sport here. Two rowing clubs use the river about this point—the University and the Printers' Rowing Clubs.'

He looked at his watch at that moment. 'Oh, I'm sorry,' he said, 'but I'll have to go. I promised my wife I'd be home for dinner at half-past twelve to-day. She's going out this afternoon.' He hesitated a moment, then went on: 'I've no wish to intrude, sir, but you mentioned some other parks that you'd like to see. If I could be of any assistance—you see, I'll be free for a day or two yet, I'd be glad to show you round.'

I jumped at the idea. 'That's extremely kind of you,' I told him, 'and I'll be delighted to have your assistance. You've made my visit to this place to-day a really pleasant one. When and where shall we meet? I'd like to go to Kelvingrove Park next.'

'Well, if this afternoon suits you, I'll be at the Kelvingrove Street entrance at 3 o'clock.'

We parted, agreeing to meet there at that time, and we met promptly. 'This is the second-oldest park in Glasgow,' he told me as we entered, 'and here is one of the oldest trees in Glasgow,' he continued, pointing to a tree. 'It's a Huntingdon willow.' 'It was a very old tree when the park came into being as such in 1852. It was one of three ancient trees, but the two others have died.' Later he showed me two rare trees, a hornbeam with a twisted stem and a fraxinus ash, which is believed to be the only one in Glasgow.

As we moved round he gave me some facts and figures about the park. Its 66 acres cost £77,945 in 1852, and when 19 acres of the lands of Clayslaps, Overnewton and Kelvinbank were bought and added in 1881 they cost over £66,000.

'I mentioned to you this forenoon,' he said, 'that previous Exhibitions had taken place here. The Art Galleries, which you've been in, were the outcome of the 1888 Exhibition, which raised part of the sum necessary for the building, although much more was subscribed in the five years that followed. The foundation stone was laid in 1897 by the Duke of York, later King George V, and the 1901 Exhibition raised £40,000 for the benefit of the art and museum collections. The building was a feature of that Exhibition. Oh, here's the duck pond! That island in it is rather interesting. It is artificial, and it's made in the shape of the island of Cyprus. It was in the news at the time, but I can't remember for what reason. There's another interesting thing in this park—a mineral well; or I should say there *was* a mineral well, for it's now dried up. I believe that at one time it was very popular with the "quality".'

From the foregoing you may be inclined to think that our conversation was devoted entirely to park matters. It was by no means so, and I found him a most interesting talker on various subjects; but as this chapter is concerned with the parks, I do not wish to introduce other matters.

We had reached the higher parts of the park, and from the high terracing we had a marvellous view of Glasgow. I felt that I wanted to come here in the dusk of a summer's evening, when the lights were beginning to glow, for I was sure that then I would see something worth while. We left Kelvingrove Park by an exit at Park Gardens, where a great granite stairway leads to Woodlands Terrace: at least, so my guide told me. He told me also that the stairway had cost £10,000, and I can well believe it.

Now, I do not wish to bore the reader with 'he said' and 'I said' throughout this chapter. Let me rather give some details, told me by good Robert B—— as he took me round the four parks I visited within the next few days.

We went first to Queen's Park, which is one of the pleasantest artificial parks I have seen.

My guide said it was the most beautiful artificial park in Glasgow, and told me also that Americans have remarked that it is the finest cultivated park they have ever seen. When you learn, as I did, that a million plants are bedded out every year, you can understand how beautifully cultivated it is. We entered the park from Victoria Road, up a granite stairway, on to a terrace which, I was told, is 750 feet long and 140 feet wide. And while we're dealing with figures, I learned also that the park originally cost £30,000 in 1857, and when Camphill was added in 1894 that addition cost £63,000.

We climbed to the flagstaff, where we had an unrivalled view of Glasgow—my guide's words —because the wind was in the south-west. The battlefield of Langside can be seen, and I learned that it was from one of the principal 'actors' in that battle, Mary Queen of Scots, that the park takes its name.

Here is another park with a museum and art gallery in it, for Camphill House serves that purpose. The house is at the base of a hill, on the crest of which is an old circular camp, some say of Caledonian origin, others, that it was Roman—hence the name Camphill. The collections in this museum are changed from time to time, thus adding a spice of variety.

Before I left this park I had a look at the old rose-garden, which must be a lovely thing in the summer; and I saw that it contained a model yachting pond, and learned that there were ten football pitches, twenty tennis courts, nine bowling greens, as well as a children's playground and a pitching and putting course.

Hogganfield Loch Park, which we visited next, is one of the newest. The loch and lands of Ruchazie, of which it is combined, were bought by Glasgow Corporation in 1920. There is an island in the loch, and it was made by 100 unemployed men engaged by the Corporation. There was a suggestion of having a bandstand on the island with a bridge across from the 'mainland,' but that didn't materialise, which seems a pity, for there is much boating in the loch; and I thought how pleasant it would be for Glasgow people to drift in little boats listening to the music from the island on a calm summer's evening. The craft to be seen on the loch in summer are rowing boats, canoes and motor boats. But you'll see no swimmers, as bathing is dangerous. And you can pitch and putt on an 18-hole course to your heart's content.

And now for Rouken Glen, which is the largest of Glasgow's parks, for it now covers 228 acres, although the original presented to Glasgow by Lord Rowallan in 1906 consisted of 135 acres. Rouken Glen is a lovely spot, and Glasgow is indeed lucky to have such a 'lung.'

If you go to Rouken Glen, provided you are lucky enough to have such an escort as I had, you will be shown the three fine trees known as 'The Three Graces,' the wall-enclosed garden and the fossils. Near the Mansion House, among the bushes, you will be shown what is believed to be part of the gateway of an old toll house. Then you will probably want to know something about the great angular piece of rock that protrudes from the steep embankment of the pathway beside the stream. It is known as the Printers' Stone, I was told. It seems that when young printers finished their apprenticeship at the nearby Thornliebank Calico Printing works, they used to come to this stone to 'pay off,' that is, stand treat to their fellow apprentices.

'There must have been some happy scenes then,' I said.

My guide smiled. 'Yes, there must have been; but there are still many happy scenes in Rouken Glen. If you could only wait until the summer, to see some of the Cripple Children's trips, they would do your heart good.'

Well, I may see these too, for there is no reason why I should leave Glasgow, except that I rarely settle anywhere for long.

And now for my last park, Victoria Park, which takes its name from the late Queen Victoria, and if you take a look at the ornamental gates, which were presented by the ladies of Partick, you will see two heads of Queen Victoria, and they are both facing the same way. This caused something of a stir, and there were protests, but the heads still look in the same direction.

Victoria Park is notable for several things. It is the only public park in Glasgow to have within it a Rugby football pitch and a shinty pitch, and it contains a fossil grove. Here ten fossilised trees and roots were discovered in 1887, and they are considered to be the finest fossilised trees ever discovered in this country.

If you prefer living trees, you will see a large plane tree with fine thick trunks. It is known as 'The Five Sisters.' And you will see a rock garden that is really a disguised quarry; and little wooden bridges spanning the ponds, and a duck pond, paddling pond, and a yachting pond.

My park prowls are ended. I shall probably see some of the other parks before I leave the city, but I cannot be certain of this. Glasgow is an extremely lucky city in respect of parks, and her citizens should be grateful to the men who had the foresight to secure them—just as I am grateful to the good Robert B—— for all his help, and for his pleasant companionship on these walks round the parks. You have not heard the last of Robert B——, for he has asked me to visit him in his home, which reminds me that I shall have to visit also my travelling-companion on the train from London when I first came to Glasgow.

Chapter XIV

I t is almost trite to say that if you wish to see
people as they really are, you must see them
in their own homes. Even there, of course, the
face that they show to the world may be main-
tained in the presence of strangers, but there is
always the chance of the mask slipping—that is,
if there is a mask, for some people are the same
always and everywhere.

Since I came to Glasgow, I have had a number of invitations to visit people I have met here.
Glasgow, as I remarked earlier, is hospitable,
but not indiscriminately so. Before a Glasgow
man invites you to his home, he has to know
you for some time; but once you are invited,
you are an honoured guest. There are excep-
tions. The man with whom I travelled to Glasgow from London gave me a warm invitation
to visit him before we parted—but, after all, we
had been in each other's company for almost
eight hours continuously—and some people I
met at a theatre one evening asked me to come
and spend the week-end at their place in the

country—this, after only about twenty minutes conversation. I declined, with the usual polite excuse of a previous engagement, but I could not help wondering what would have happened if I had accepted that invitation. My hosts would probably have spent the best part of the week-end puzzling out 'who this fellow is,' and I should have felt uncomfortable.

I am really a reluctant guest, and even more so if I am asked to spend a day or two with people. Years of knocking about the world have not cured me of this reluctance to stay with friends or acquaintances at their homes. The mornings are my bugbear.

You are asked for the week-end, and you arrive on Saturday afternoon in time for lunch. That over, you have a round of golf with your host, or allow him to arrange your afternoon and evening as he thinks fit. And at night, after a pleasant day, you say, as you make for your bedroom, 'When's breakfast?'

I always dread the reply to that question, for as often as not it is 'Oh, any old time on Sunday. Just please yourself—unless, of course, you'd prefer it in bed.'

I never prefer it in bed. I loathe it in bed. Despite the advanced state of civilisation, no one has yet devised a perfect method of breakfasting in bed. I meet people who say they have discovered such a method; I give it a trial—and I am no better off. It is a pity, for breakfast in bed would solve my greatest problem as a guest, the problem arising out of 'Oh, any old time on Sunday.'

What happens to me is this. I wake early, and discover that my watch has stopped. It always seems to stop in strange houses. The state of the light indicates that the morning is well advanced. I lie and listen for sounds of life, but the house is still, and not a soul seems to be stirring.

I lie thus for what seems like hours, and, just as I decide to turn over and try to sleep again, a clock strikes—once! It is a quarter-past something. But what? Probably quarter-past eight, or nine, or, horrible thought, it may be a quarter-past ten. My mind refuses to entertain the idea that it can possibly be quarter-past eleven, and that my host and hostess have breakfasted, and are cursing me for upsetting their day. That thought, unfortunately, keeps butting in. I can see and hear it all. My hostess, whom I do not know very well, says to her husband: 'Your friend isn't a very good riser. Breakfast will be ruined if we wait any longer. Don't you think you might give him a call?'

My host thinks the same, but hates to admit it. 'Oh, the poor chap is bound to be tired. The country air, and his journey down yesterday, you know. Better let him sleep for a bit yet. We'll just carry on.'

His wife agrees, somewhat reluctantly, and they breakfast in silence, she thinking that her husband's friend *might* have tried to be on time, or agreed to have his breakfast in bed; he thinking that it was all dashed awkward, and hoping that Mary wasn't going to be peeved about it.

All this and more goes through my mind, and then the clock strikes the half-hour. But half-past what? The next half-hour is torture. Several times I get up, tip-toe to the door and open it quietly, listening for any sounds of life in the house. There is not a sound, except the ticking of the clock in the hall, and I have the mad idea of creeping downstairs to see the time. Then I realise that I'd hate to be caught creeping downstairs, for the breakfast-room door would be sure to open, and my hostess would assume a geniality that she did not feel, and say something about it being perfectly all right.

Why the devil did I allow myself to be per-

suaded to come here at all? I must have been
mad. Then I suddenly discover that I cannot
hear the ticking of the clock. Heavens! Has it
stopped? Luckily, at that moment, it strikes the
three-quarters. Only another fifteen minutes,
and I shall know the worst. I go back to bed,
and I'm cold now. I lie there, miserable, while
time marches on about as speedily as a fully
dressed deep-sea diver would walk across a
ploughed field. At last, when I feel that I shall
have to stuff the blankets into my mouth in case
I scream the house down, the clock strikes—six!

In the end, I lie awake for the next few hours,
or go to sleep, only to be wakened by my host
thundering at the door and shouting something
about 'old sleepyhead.' Can you wonder that I
am a reluctant guest?

This won't do, I'm afraid. I began this chapter with the intention of saying something about
Glasgow hospitality in general, and two inci-
dents in particular. Yet I have rambled on
about my problems as a guest. I promise to
stick to the point from now on.

I wish to put on record something about two
invitations I accepted. The first came from my
friend of the London-Glasgow train, the second
from Robert B——, who had been so helpful to

me in the tour of the parks. My hosts were entirely different from each other; one was rich and lived in the West End, the other was a working-man who lived in the East End. Yet both had one thing in common—a sense of real hospitality.

Let me tell you about my visits. I was asked to tea by Robert B——; and tea, in Glasgow, as I have mentioned earlier in this book, is not tea as we know it elsewhere. It is a meal, a substantial meal, and often consists of two courses. I had accepted Robert B——'s invitation on one condition—that my visit made no difference to the normal procedure of his wife or himself. I hate to upset people's arrangements, and besides, I want to see things as they really are, 'warts and all,' as Cromwell said to the artist who was painting his portrait.

Robert B—— and his wife lived in a flat, or tenement house, above a shop. Their house consisted of two rooms and a kitchen which I reached after entering a close and climbing some flights of stairs. The stairs had been newly washed, and a wet pipe-clay odour filled the close.

The shining nameplate on the door, and the equally shining bell handle, told me at once that Mrs. B—— (whom I had not yet met) was a good housewife, as she turned out to be. Robert himself opened the door, welcomed me warmly, and equally welcome was the delicious smell of cooking that pervaded the small hall— they referred to it as lobby. 'Come away ben,' said Robert when I had disposed of my coat and hat in the lobby, and I was ushered into the kitchen, and introduced to Mrs. B——.

Mrs. B—— turned out to be exactly as I had pictured her. She was a buxom, fresh-complexioned woman of fifty or a little more. Her dark hair was greying slightly, but her face was smooth. 'It's an awful-like thing to ask you to your tea in the kitchen,' she said, 'but Robert wouldn't let me set it in the parlour.'

'I'm glad he was so firm about it,' I replied. 'I'd much prefer to have it here.'

While the good lady busied herself with final preparations for tea, I sat in an easy chair at the fireside. It was an old chair that had seen good service, but it was unusually comfortable. I was able to take stock of the kitchen as I sat there, and I doubt if I've ever seen any place that shone like it. At the end of a shelf, well stocked with dishes, stood a large metal pan, the inside of which shone like burnished gold.

I'm really very ignorant about such matters, and I wish you could have seen the look of surprise on Mrs. B——'s face when, in answer to my query, she said: 'It's a jelly-pan.' I have an idea that her first thought was that I was joking. Underneath the shelf hung a row of brightly polished dish-covers, and every piece of metal in that kitchen shone and sparkled. The grate and all about it—fender, trivet, kettles—could not possibly have been cleaner, and even the very canary, that occupied an equally shining brass cage, hanging near the window, seemed to realise its good luck, for it sang lustily. Actually, the reason for its singing, I learned, was something much more prosaic. It could hear ham frying in the scullery, which always made it burst into song. The rest of the kitchen was in keeping. A bright linoleum, and bright rugs, covered the floor; a wag-at-the-wa' clock ticked comfortably on the wall; a sofa stood before a curtained recess—a concealed bed—and a dresser ran along one side of the kitchen, a dresser on which stood two little cupboards and some trays. The wall opposite the window was occupied by some bookshelves, under which was a small chest of drawers, on which a plant stood. A china dog sat at each end of the mantelpiece, on which were also two brass candlesticks and a tea-caddy.

Mrs. B—— came out of the scullery, removing her overall. 'Tea's ready,' she said; 'you sit here, Mr. Gulliver, and—and—take off your jacket if you like and make yourself at home.' My good friend Robert, however, retained his jacket, so I kept mine on—but I had a feeling that I might have been better to have removed it—if only Robert had given a lead. I'm sure he always removed his.

'It's ham and haddie,' said Mrs. B——, as she put a generous plateful before me. 'I hope you like it; it's real tasty.'

'There's nothing I like better,' I replied, although the dish was new to me. I have since learned that it is a favourite dish in Glasgow, and elsewhere in Scotland.

It is altogether delectable: if for nothing else, it was worth coming to Glasgow to discover such a dish. What genius evolved it I do not know, but the combination of fried smoked ham and haddock is perfect, as perfect as the wedding of bacon and eggs.

What a meal that was! Your gourmet might not have approved, but what did that matter? A heaped plateful of home-baked scones quickly disappeared—'eat up, Mr. Gulliver, there's plenty more'—and there were cookies and buns, cakes, a large piece of sultana cake, and two kinds of home-made jam, both of which I sampled. One was bramble jelly, and I shall not taste its like again, I feel certain. One other thing stands out from that glorious meal—cap biscuits and carvy. The cap biscuit is a plain biscuit with a raised rim round it. This is generously spread with fresh butter, over which is sprinkled the carvy—caraway seeds encased in sugar—and I know of nothing quite like this delicious tit-bit. I am told that it was much more common in Scotland years ago than it now is, and that it is not seen in many homes to-day; so I was in luck.

That mighty tea came to an end at last and, as Mrs. B—— cleared away, and washed up in the scullery, I inspected Robert's bookshelves. I knew that I would find several volumes of Carlyle there—I noticed that the *Life of John Sterling* was well thumbed—and I expected a Burns and some Scott. The Journals of the last-named also had a well-read look, and I found that Robert admired them tremendously. There was a Shakespeare, a Longfellow, Emerson's Essays, two volumes of Hazlitt,

Lamb's Essays, Dr. John Brown's Letters, the Table Talk of Samuel Rogers, Alexander Smith's *A Summer in Skye* and *Dreamthorp*, Macaulay's Essays, Boswell's *Johnson*, Macdonald's *Rambles Round Glasgow* and *Days at the Coast*, the Barsetshire novels of Anthony Trollope, *Wild Life in a Southern County*, and *The Amateur Poacher* by Richard Jefferies, some Dickens, William de Morgan's *Joseph Vance*, the Travels of Mungo Park, White's *Natural History of Selborne*, Bates's *Naturalist on the Amazon*, and Oliver Wendell Holmes's *Autocrat of the Breakfast Table*. I cannot remember any others, except three modern books—Wells's *Short History of the World*, Tomlinson's *The Sea and the Jungle* and Kenneth Grahame's *The Wind in the Willows*. The last one surprised me, yet I found that it was among the favourites.

'And this is grand stuff,' he said, as he pulled the Tomlinson out. 'Man, if there's one place on earth I want to see before I die it's the Amazon. I know the world's an interesting place, and there's lots of it a man should see, but I'm not caring about the rest of it if I could see the Amazon. Tomlinson's book put me on to Bates, and I've read some others from the public library. But I don't suppose I'll ever see the

Amazon—but I expect you think I'm daft,' and he laughed rather self-consciously.

At that moment Mrs. B—— entered, just in time to hear his last words. She laughed. 'Him and his old Amazon,' she said, 'he's got it on the brain.' But I think she understood.

For the next two hours we smoked our pipes and talked, while Mrs. B—— knitted, and threw in an occasional word. We talked about his books, of which he was justifiably proud—I found the diversity of his reading remarkable, and said so—and we talked about the present condition of the world. Both Robert and his wife took a lively interest in affairs, and were intelligent readers of the newspapers. Little by little I learned that he was happy in his work and his home—the latter was obvious—and was content with his lot, as long as he was able to have his tobacco, and an occasional shilling or two to buy a few books, mostly from the barrows. He and his wife, although he gave her all the credit, had managed to save a little money, and their only regret was that they had no family. Mrs. B——'s chief interest, after her husband and her house, was, I gathered, a mysterious something, known as 'the Guild' where she met other ladies, and enjoyed herself.

I told them a little about my travels—unfortunately I had not sailed on the Amazon—but I spoke as little as possible, as I wanted to listen rather than talk. The time passed quickly, and when I looked at my watch it was half-past nine. I made to rise, and that was the signal for Mrs. B——. 'You're not going out of this house to-night without a cup of tea,' she said, and would take no denial, despite my protests. 'The kettle's on,' was her only other remark, and that seemed to clinch the matter. I had to have more tea.

When I did eventually take my leave, it was to the accompaniment of 'You'll come back again soon,' and 'We've been awful pleased to see you.'

I was touched by this genuine expression of goodwill, and by this hospitality to a stranger. It was an evening I shall never forget, for I had been given something that cannot be bought, and I was almost afraid to visit my West End acquaintance lest the contrast be disappointing. That other visit will require a chapter to itself.

Chapter XV

One of the things I discovered shortly after I came to Glasgow was that there is supposed to be a bitter rivalry between this city and Edinburgh. The first hint I got of this was in a music-hall one evening, when a comedian made a 'slighting' reference to Edinburgh, and his remark was greeted with hearty laughter. 'That's one in the eye to Edinburgh,' said a man on my right, and his companion agreed—just as the comedian said slyly: 'I cracked that joke in Edinburgh last week, only about Glasgow, and they laughed louder there!'

Several times since then I've noticed that when Glasgow and Edinburgh men get together they delight in making jokes against each other's city.

'Do you really dislike Edinburgh and Edinburgh people?' I asked one Glasgow man of my acquaintance.

'Not really,' he replied laughing, 'but there's

just a feeling, a sort of undercurrent you might call it. It's the sort of thing that often exists between cities. Glasgow people are supposed to regard Edinburgh as a city of pride and poverty, while there is said to be a feeling in Edinburgh that Glasgow has no culture, and that all we think about is commerce and money-making. Actually, I think the whole thing is nonsense, and that no such feelings exist; but we both pretend that it does, and we keep it up. It's really akin to the joke about Scottish meanness. Scotsmen aren't mean, but they love to keep alive the legend of the canny bang-goes-saxpence Scot. You'll find that if you visit Edinburgh, the people there are every bit as pleasant and hospitable as the Glasgow folk. And you've been long enough in Glasgow now to realise that we are not entirely a city of money-grubbers.'

That is perfectly true. Glasgow is a great industrial city but it has not lost its soul. Even to the visitor—as I have indicated in preceding chapters—its very real interest in the arts is obvious. This interest is not confined to any particular class, but is general. I have already told you about my visit to the home of Robert B——, of his books and his general outlook on life. Let me tell you something about my visit to Mr. McMungo—that is not his real name, by the way—one of Glasgow's leading industrialists and, I suppose, one of the money-grubbers referred to. Mr. McMungo was my fellow-traveller from London when I came to Glasgow. You may recall that when we parted at the Central Station he gave me his cards—business address and home—and asked me to give him a ring one day. Well, I 'phoned him at his office, and was immediately asked to lunch with him at his club, an invitation that I accepted gladly, for I felt that I might meet several of Mr. McMungo's friends, and I wished to 'get an angle,' as the newspaper men say, on the big business men of Glasgow.

Well, I met some of them in the smoking-room after lunch, and on this and subsequent visits I never once heard the big business men mention business. They were all men of some position, important men in industry, but they had many other interests. You, who may know these men, may wonder at my remarking on this: but I have met many big business men in other parts of the world, and almost the only topic of conversation they had was business. In Glasgow, this seems to be confined to works, offices and boardrooms: at least, that is my impression.

Mr. McMungo was eager to hear my impressions of Glasgow, but the club smoking-room was not the best place for a conversation of this kind on this particular day.

'Why not dine with me one night?' said Mr. McMungo. 'How are you placed this week?'

'My nights are my own,' I told him, 'and any one that suits you suits me.'

'Good,' said he, 'tomorrow it is. I'll lift you at the hotel at five o'clock. We dine at six, so that anyone who wishes to go to a theatre has time for a meal first.'

Promptly at five o'clock the following evening Mr. McMungo called for me, and quarter of an hour later we were passing the Botanic Gardens —which I have not yet visited—and were making our way out Great Western Road, off which we turned later to the McMungo home. Great Western Road, along which I have travelled several times in a less luxurious fashion—Mr. McMungo's car is a Rolls Royce— is a magnificent thoroughfare. No other city that I have seen has such a fine approach to it as this Great Western Road. Beautiful and dignified houses and terraces of houses stand on each side. It was easy to see that this had been the West End for a considerable time, for outside many of the houses was a stepping stone used in the days when carriages were the thing. It was pleasant to see these reminders of the past still there.

A minute after turning out of Great Western Road, we drew up before a substantial mansion standing in a fair-sized piece of ground. There was a delightful lawn at the back and side of the house, a well-kept garden and shrubbery, and everything spoke of wealth and comfort, an impression that was confirmed by the interior of the house. The quiet dignity of the place was impressive. The hall was spacious, and might have been sombre had it not been for the generous fire that burned in a huge grate. Every hall—that is, every hall in a large house—should have a fireplace, and a fire in it as long as the weather demands it. I know of nothing so welcoming as a fire in the hall, and there is at least one theatre in Glasgow that boasts a vestibule fire. I'm certain it helps to draw the crowd.

We were welcomed by Mrs. McMungo in the drawing-room upstairs. She was a charming woman in a charming room. Drawing-rooms to me are usually detestable places, full of uncomfortable furniture and innumerable bits and pieces. Here, however, comfort predominated, a comfort that was enhanced by the warmth of my welcome by everybody, for, in addition to Mrs. McMungo were her two daughters and her son.

Dinner was a plain, appetising meal, with no frills. It was typical of what I have noticed since I came to Glasgow. Your Glasgow man is not a big eater. He may occasionally have a celebration and dine and wine expensively, but his dinner usually consists of soup, joint and a simple sweet, such as apple tart, while his lunch very often is made of one course, with perhaps a biscuit and cheese to follow.

We drank an excellent claret with our dinner. 'I like claret for itself,' said Mr. McMungo; 'but I like to think I am drinking the wine that was drunk by our Scottish forefathers. You may not know, Mr. Gulliver, that it was at one time the favourite drink in Scotland—they drank it even at breakfast in the old days.'

'I shouldn't like to drink it at breakfast today,' said young McMungo, laughingly. 'It would be horrible—even this claret of yours, father.'

'Ah, Scotsmen aren't what they were,' said his father: 'although I agree with you, my boy. I shouldn't like it either.'

We had our coffee in the music room, a delightful room in the shape of an 'L' that led off the dining room. Here, too, comfort was the keynote—that seems the appropriate word for such a room—and one of my host's daughters sat down at the piano soon afterwards and played some Mozart in a way that surprised me. I must have shown my surprise, for her father said: 'She was trained in Germany and she's had lessons from two famous pianists.'

The younger generation of McMungos had an engagement, and left us about eight o'clock. We settled down at the fireside, and as I looked at my host on one side and my hostess, with her sewing, on the other, I could not help recalling my visit to my other, and more humble, friend Robert B——. The social positions of my two hosts were poles apart, yet my welcome and entertainment had no essential difference. Both treated me as if they were really glad to have me; both gave me of their best; and both were sterling examples of the real Glasgow man.

'Well, tell me what you think of Glasgow

and Glasgow people?' said Mr. McMungo, and I related, briefly, many of the things that I have related in this book.

'But what of the gangs and the wild men, and the mud huts, and the dirt, and all the other things you were to find, according to your friends?' he asked, with a smile, when I had finished.

'Well, I've seen no gangs or wild men,' I said: 'and I'd hardly call your beautiful buildings, and such houses as this, mud huts. As for dirt—well, I've seen parts of Glasgow that seem disgraceful to me—every city seems to have such parts—but, at the same time, if all I read in your newspapers is correct, a gallant attempt is being made to improve such conditions.'

'Yes, something is being done: probably more than people realise; but there's a great deal to do yet. Employers in a big way, and I am one, are often regarded as ogres, but believe me, I am anything but an ogre. I have the greatest respect for the Glasgow working-man— Why shouldn't I? My own great grandfather was himself a working smith. We have a few "outsiders" who stir up unnecessary trouble— and outsiders don't belong to any particular class—but for honesty, good workmanship and good fellowship, I'll put your Glasgow working-man against any other in Britain. And I don't say that lightly.'

'I'm glad to hear your impressions,' broke in Mrs. McMungo, looking up from her sewing. 'So many people have an entirely wrong impression of Glasgow and its people. My husband tells me that you are going to write about Glasgow. I'm glad of that too, for you will be able to write impartially, and, from what you've told us, you have been favourably impressed.'

'Hear, hear!' said her husband: 'and I think we should have a drink on the strength of that, Gulliver.' With that he crossed to a small table on which a tray with decanters and bottles stood, filled out generous pegs for us both, and we drank to the future of Glasgow.

Our talk became general after that, and I found that my host had a wide knowledge of the arts. Music was his particular passion, and, being a wealthy man, he could indulge himself. He had been several times to the Salzburg Festival, and spoke with knowledge of the conducting of Bruno Walter and various other eminent conductors. He had heard all the leading artistes of note on the opera stage or concert platform, and his criticisms of this player or that singer were just and balanced, or seemed so to me.

I found, too, that he was an enthusiastic bookman, and his library was a living thing to him and not merely a collection of expensively bound books. He had some modern first editions that made me envy him—Maugham's *Of Human Bondage*, Bennett's *Old Wives' Tale*, some Galsworthy's (under the name of Sinjohn) and one or two others, all of which he had bought on their original appearance. That, however, did not apply to some very early Kiplings, for which he had paid a stiff price, as he had also for a Conrad which contained some imperfection that made it valuable. He did not, however, collect books merely for their value. He knew his books, and got the greatest pleasure from them. I found that we shared an enthusiasm for Lamb, Austin Dobson, and Anthony Trollope—his knowledge of the Barsetshire novels was complete, and I found that he knew even the more obscure Trollopes

His pictures I cannot describe, for the simple reason that I know too little about the modern school of painters to write about them. All I can say is that he justified everything that was on his walls, for he knew much about their painters and what they did and had attempted to do. Throughout all this, there was never a hint of boastfulness because of his possessions. All these valuable things gave him the right kind of pleasure, and he appreciated his good fortune at being able to have them.

You must not think, however, that my host's interests were purely literary and artistic. He had travelled much, and his knowledge of affairs, national and international, was wide. He had his prejudices—some of them unjust, I thought—and no doubt many faults that I was not aware of, for I did not know him intimately. Yet if I were asked to sum him up in a few words, I should describe him as a cultured, clever man; a good employer and a good citizen.

You may say that I have been lucky in the people I've met in Glasgow. I have—but I refuse to believe that they are exceptional.

Chapter XVI

Turning over the pages of a little volume of poems by a Scots poet, Alexander Smith, I came on a poem entitled ' Glasgow.' Two lines of that poem stood out from the others, and have lingered in my mind. Here they are:

> *Instead of shores where ocean beats*
> *I hear the ebb and flow of streets.*

The ebb and flow of streets! What a complete description lies in these few words! They set me thinking about Glasgow streets in general and three in particular; for in these three streets, Glasgow life is reflected almost completely. Each has its own characteristics, and each I found so intensely interesting that I made it my business to find out something about all of them. What I found out, plus my own observations, may be of interest to the stranger who chances to read this book; and even to the Glasgow reader.

My three streets are Sauchiehall Street, Buchanan Street and Argyle Street, and the greatest of these is Sauchiehall Street. By 'greatest' I mean that it *is* Glasgow. I heard someone describe it as 'the Princes Street of Glasgow,' to which came the retort, 'No, Princes Street is the Sauchiehall Street of Edinburgh.' As to that, I cannot judge, for at the moment of writing I have not yet seen Princes Street or Edinburgh.

The origin of the name is debated, but the likeliest one, given me by a man interested in such things, is that this street is built on what was once a 'haugh' or meadow where the saugh trees (willows) wept. It is difficult to imagine to-day that this very busy thoroughfare was ever a meadow, but all of our towns must have been at one time simply country.

I must warn you that it is with only part of Sauchiehall Street that I intend to deal—the part between Renfield Street and Charing Cross. It is considerably longer than that. Past Charing Cross it becomes a street of private houses, in many of which doctors reside and consult. There are terraces of them and in these terraces will be found offices, dentists, show-rooms for furs, clothes, and so on. No doubt this part of Sauchiehall Street has a life peculiarly its own, but it is more a life behind doors than in the street itself. There is also the lower end of the street—a not very exciting part, although it contains two theatres and a famous restaurant.

The corner of Renfield Street and Sauchiehall Street is a famous corner. To be strictly correct there are four corners, the most famous of which is Simpson's Corner. It is on the lower side and on the left as you come out of Renfield Street, and takes its name from a music-seller's there. I learned that it was at one time the best-known rendezvous in Glasgow. Opposite it, at any of the other three corners, but particularly on the other side of Sauchiehall Street, you will see quite often little groups of actors from the nearby theatres and music-halls standing.

The time to see Sauchiehall Street at its best is in the afternoon; and if the weather is fine, the street presents a gay and busy picture. It was really an amazing street, for in addition to its luxury shops, its cinemas, and its dance-halls, it contained a tombstone yard! A splendid new hotel has arisen on the site of that rather grim place which recalled the pleasant habit of the ancient Egyptians of dragging a mummified body through the banqueting hall at a feast, so that the diners would be reminded that they were mortal no matter how much they enjoyed eating, drinking and being merry.

I don't suppose anybody ever gave the tombstone yard a thought in Sauchiehall Street. It had been there so long that it had become part of the streetscape, and it is probably much more noticed now that it is removed—which seems to me a particularly Irish way of saying it.

The shops in Sauchiehall Street are—well, visiting actresses, film stars and Americans say 'I think your shops are wonderful,' instead of giving their opinion about the policemen. That gives you an idea of the shops. And some of them are more than mere shops, for these huge warehouses extend for a considerable length and height, and I should say that a window-cleaner's job there is a permanent one. A woman can spend the best part of the day in Sauchiehall Street looking in at the windows, and they are certainly worth looking in at. 'Beckoning fair ones' (in wax) attract the eye— how much more lifelike wax figures have become in recent years!—and I have watched many women before a window that contained nothing but a single hat. That single hat idea struck me as good. It showed so very little, yet it seemed to say: 'This hat, as you can see, is very smart. But it's really nothing to what we have inside. What about it?' Yes, the single hat is sound psychology. You can live a complete life in Sauchiehall Street. You can buy everything for eating that you can want, necessity and luxury. You can dance, go to the pictures in two senses, for there is also an art gallery—the MacLellan Galleries—and you can buy clothes, footwear, hats, jewellery; have your hair waved and your teeth drawn; and you can furnish your house completely, even to flowers. A man I met told me that when he and his wife were young and none too well off, they sometimes walked up and down Sauchiehall Street 'furnishing' their house—the one they were to have when their ship came home—and spending several thousands on the furniture. It was a harmless and pleasant game. And I must put on record that the best toasted muffins I have ever eaten I got in Sauchiehall Street. Where? Ah, that would be telling. If everybody knew, the toasted muffins might not remain the best, and a man who stumbles on a treasure of this kind is a fool if he talks too much about it.

So much for Sauchiehall Street; let's take a look at Buchanan Street. I should say that this is Glasgow's most dignified street—that is, the part of it that is interesting to shoppers. Buchanan Street rises, and as it rises it dwindles. Only once have I ventured to the dwindling point that ends in Buchanan Street Station, and I have no desire to see that part of it again. It may be reeking with interest for all I know; it may contain fascinating things that I did not see. I care not: 'I did not like its ugly face.'

There is one little point about Buchanan Street that should be cleared up, and that is the correct pronunciation of its name. One man calls it Buck-anan another Bew-canan, and each swears he is right.

The street, which was opened in 1780, I have found out, is named after a certain Andrew Buchanan, who was at one time a leading merchant in the city. Andrew had four acres of ground that extended from St. Enoch Burn on the south to Gordon Street on the north, and on this ground the first Buchanan Street came into being. The northern part of the street was not built until twenty-four years later, and now the entire street is one.

It's a fashionable street—the most fashionable in Glasgow, if one judges by the number of cars one sees standing at the kerb, in which sit waiting chauffeurs in livery. Expensive cars predominate, and there is a real air of affluence about this street. Did I not see a pair of gloves in a window here priced at £8? That gives you an idea.

The street is wide, and the shop or warehouse windows are also wide. The shoddy article or tawdry finery are not to be found here.

While the high part of Buchanan Street did not interest me, as I have told you, the short stretch immediately on the north side of St. Vincent Street did. In that short stretch you will find the Stock Exchange—where all the good stories are said to originate—St. George's Church, in the tower of which is one of Glasgow's most popular clocks—at least, I am told so—and the Athenaeum, and the Scottish National Academy of Music. But that, I think, is probably all you want to know about Buchanan Street.

Argyle Street is completely different from either of these two others. It is the street of the people, and it is usually crowded. I could swear that no one has ever seen it completely empty; I doubt if it ever has been. As a rule it is usually seething with a mass of people, and if you would see it at its best, visit it on a Saturday night. I had heard of Argyle Street long before I saw it, and heard of it in the strangest places: for if two Glasgow engineers should meet in a foreign port, one is almost certain to ask about Argyle Street, and before long you will hear them swapping yarns about this street on a Saturday night.

Again, I am not dealing with the entire street, but simply that part between the Trongate and Union Street. Argyle Street stretches far after it passes Union Street, but it loses its character then, and becomes simply a street. The crowds are confined to the section with which I deal. And what crowds! It is sometimes difficult to walk here. The street might be summed up in—crowds, crowds, crowds, against a background of clanging tramcars, cries of street vendors, and excitement. For the first time in my life I was asked to buy a suit of clothes here. I had stopped for a moment to look in at a tailor's window— more to have a rest than to view his goods. Before I could turn away, a polite young man in black jacket, striped trousers, and wearing a bowler hat, took my arm and suggested that I could do with a new suit. 'We have,' he said, 'some very natty suitings inside.' I protested, rather feebly, I admit, for I am a bad protester in such circumstances, and but for the fact that my young fellow's attention was distracted for a moment, I should now be the possessor of a suit that I did not want.

Of a certain author it was said that you cannot fail to be thrilled by his novels. Well, you cannot fail to be thrilled by Argyle Street. It is full of gusto. It could not be dull if it tried.

'It's not what it was,' said a man with whom I got into conversation—no place ever is— 'but it's still a grand street. I remember when there were lots of dulse barrows, and I used to buy dulse, and whelks and cockles. You don't know what dulse is? My dear sir, it's a kind of seaweed that's good to eat. Fine salty stuff. I was forbidden to buy it—but I bought it all right. And whelks, too; although I expect you call them winkles. What, you've never eaten them! Gosh! You haven't lived if you've never picked a whelk out of its shell with a pin!'

I'm afraid my education, in some respects, has been sadly neglected.

Here, I think, a spot of history might be given. Argyle Street is one of the oldest thoroughfares in Glasgow. It has had many names. In 1124 it was the road to Dumbarton Castle, and was known as Dumbarton Road.

Later it became Wester Gate, then Anderston Walk, and finally Argyle Street. That was round about the end of the eighteenth century, for the first record of its being known as Argyle Street was in 1783. The story goes that the body of Archibald, third Duke of Argyle, who died in England in 1761, lay in state at the Black Bull Inn, then known as the Highland Society's House. The name is said to commemorate this event, but no one has traced the use of the name before July 27, 1783. On that particular date, one, 'R. Browne, perfumer, Argyle Street,' had an advertisement inserted in the public press that he sold genuine violet powder for the hair. So R. Browne takes his place, even if it is a very minor one, in the history of Glasgow.

Nothing remains of the Black Bull Inn today except a plaque to remind citizens that it once existed. You will find it on the walls of a warehouse at the corner of Argyle Street and Virginia Street. On it there is no mention of the Duke, but it tells us that Robert Burns lodged here when the building was the Black Bull Inn. The poet visited Glasgow in June 1787, and in February and March 1788.

Remember, too, as you look into the innumerable shop windows, that it was in Argyle Street that the first plate-glass window ever seen in Glasgow was put in by a Virginia Street plumber in 1828. It is on record that the people laughed at him—but pioneers were always treated thus.

Let us make our way through the crowds towards the Union Street end. Leave the street for a little and enter the arcade that runs in an L shape between Argyle Street and Buchanan Street. You will notice, if you are observant, that it is the Argyll and not the Argyle Arcade. I wonder why? Nobody could tell me.

This arcade must be a paradise for small boys. Several shops offer model aeroplanes for sale, and one shop is full of model ships and yachts, and all that goes with them. I confess to spending a considerable time here myself.

There is a legend that shortly after this Arcade was opened, an officer of militia rode a horse through it for a bet. It must have been less busy in those days.

Come out of the Arcade, and push on to the busiest corner in Glasgow—Argyle Street, Jamaica Street and Union Street. You will pass a Dickensian tavern and restaurant where, it is claimed, the first Welsh rarebit was made.

So this is Glasgow!

Whether this was the first in the world, or the first in Glasgow, I have not been able to find out. All I do know is that they are still good. Pass Union Street, and you are approaching a part of Argyle Street that would be in perpetual darkness if it were not that artificial light is kept burning all the time. This part of the street is under the L.M.&S. railway bridge, a bridge that is known as the Highlanders' Umbrella. Tradition has it that the lads and lasses from the Isles meet there on their nights off.

Chapter XVII

If I might adapt the saying, 'Give a dog a
bad name and hang it,' I should say, 'Give
a bridge a good name and ignore it.' That's
how it would go in Glasgow. By 'it' I mean the
name, not the bridge. Probably the best-known
bridge in Glasgow is Glasgow Bridge, but the
chances are that if you mentioned Glasgow
Bridge to a Glasgow man he would not know
which bridge you meant. Mention Jamaica
Bridge, and that's another matter. Yet these
two bridges are the same bridge, and as it is an
extension of Jamaica Street, Glasgow Bridge is
known solely as Jamaica Bridge.

My first view of this bridge was a rather surprising one. It was packed from end to end with
tramcars and buses. Apart from the pavements,
there was nothing to be seen but a row of trams
and buses pointing south and a row of each
pointing north. Some sort of hold-up had
occurred, and this solid mass of vehicles stood
on the bridge, as if the B.B.C. announcer of 'In
Town To-night' had cried 'Stop!' My chief

thought was 'How can this structure possibly bear this tremendous weight? Did the builders foresee that one day it would be asked to do so, and build an especially strong bridge?' As nobody seemed to see anything unusual about it, I needn't have worried. So when, at last, the traffic moved on, I strode to the parapet and looked down at the Broomielaw. There was not much to be seen except a short stretch of dirty river, with a little quay on the right completely overshadowed by a huge railway bridge. 'This *is* the Broomielaw?' I said to a man who stood beside me, and gazed at the water, as if fascinated.

'Oh, ay,' he said, 'it's the Broomielaw all right, but no' the Broomielaw that Glasgow knows to-day. I fancy that you might call this the original Broomielaw, that wee quay there, but the steamers leave from further down the river. If you want to see it, you'll have to cut along there to the George V Bridge. I'm going that way if you like to come.'

I thanked him and said that I should. Before we turned away, however, he pointed to the dirty river that flowed beneath us. 'Man, you wouldn't think it was runnin' through orchards a wee while ago. I was up the river at the weekend, and it was a sight for sore eyes. You should have a look at it before the blossom fades. It's the grandest sight in Scotland just now.'

We made our way along the riverside, under the railway bridge, and soon were at the George V Bridge. Here, indeed, one could see the river for some length, and the sight of a great river such as the Clyde, with its long wharves, its warehouses, cranes, and ships, never fails to stir me. Here is the stuff of romance, for up and down this strip of water move the ships of the world; ships that have tossed on 'perilous seas forlorn' and have visited the remote places of the earth. I'm afraid that I have an incurably romantic streak in me that my knocking about the world has not eliminated.

My companion of the minute was more practical. 'You should see this place in the summer,' he said, indicating the bridge parapet; 'it's packed with people watching all that goes on down below on the river. And there's lots to see. Over on the left there the river steamers leave for the Firth. If you get a chance you should sail down the river. These are the Irish boats on the right—that big fellow there is one of the new Belfast boats—but the smaller one astern is the Campbeltown boat. She's the

Davaar, and a bonnie ship she is. Many's the time I've sailed in her. You know, mister, you *ought* to take a sail down the river!'

'I've been on the Firth,' I told him: 'I took the train to Gourock, and sailed to Rothesay.'

'It's a grand sail, right enough,' said he, 'but it's no' the same as a sail from here to Greenock.'

'What are these two boats doing in the middle of the river?' I asked him, pointing to what looked like a dredger, accompanied by another craft.

'That's a dredger working at the river bed,' he said. 'They've got to keep at it all the time or the channel would fill up. That's a bucket dredger, scooping away at the bottom of the river, and all the mud and silt that comes up is put into the other boat—it's called a hopper— and when she's full up, away she goes down to the deep waters of the Firth and dumps her cargo. You can always tell when a dredger's working in the river. See these three black balls at the mast-head? There's two on one side of the mast and one on the other. Well, any vessel that wants to pass that dredger must do so on the side that the two black balls are showing. Man, it must be great to have a job on one of these boats. You're there for life if you like to stay.'

He said it so wistfully, and with such a feeling of longing in his voice, that I felt he was a somewhat disappointed man. Personally, such a job would tend to grow monotonous.

'I wish you could see this place in summer,' said my companion again, as we made to leave: 'you've no idea what it's like. You should be here when the poor mothers and children are having their annual sail down the river as guests of the Corporation. Man, it would do your heart good. And you should see it at Glasgow Fair, with the crowds making for the coast and the Irish boats. This is nothing.'

We made our way along Midland Street, a rather depressing little street, redeemed by a famous hostelry at the Jamaica Street end. I asked my companion if he would care to 'have one,' and he accepted the invitation gladly. As we lingered over our drinks, he enquired if I was remaining in Glasgow to see the Exhibition, and when I said that I might, it led him on to an interesting reminiscence. 'The Broomielaw that we've just been looking at is gey dirty,' he said, 'but it's nothing to what it was. It's talking about the Exhibition that reminded me of

175

something that happened at the Exhibition of 1901: not actually at the Exhibition, but connected with it. I was a young fellow then, and we were living in Greenock at the time. An uncle of mine had come home from South Africa for a holiday, and, naturally, he wanted to see the Exhibition. We could have gone by train, but nothing would do but that we should sail up the Clyde. In those days the upper reaches were decidedly smelly, and although it's nearly forty years ago, I can smell the river yet. It was a blazing hot day in July, and as soon as we reached the upper part of the river, it began to hum. If you've ever smelt a glue factory in full blast or a chemical works, you'll have some idea of what it was like, provided you multiply it by twelve. I saw my uncle beginning to turn green under his tan, and although he was an almost fanatical teetotaller, the first thing he did when he stepped off the steamer was to go into a public-house and swallow a neat glass of brandy. They must have been stout fellows in those days who sailed regularly in the steamers from the Broomielaw. Everything's changed now: there's never a whiff from the river: at least, not at any time I've sailed on it in recent years.

'Well, once again, sir, here's your very good health,' said he, lifting his glass and draining it. We parted soon afterwards, he happy to have been able to tell a stranger something about Glasgow, and I extremely grateful for all the information I had received. Before I left him, I was firmly resolved to have a sail down the river, as far as Greenock. For one thing, I wished to see the *Queen Elizabeth*, then on the stocks at John Brown's yard. I could only hope that I would be as lucky then in meeting an informative companion as I had been on Jamaica Bridge. Believe it or not, my luck held in this respect.

My self-appointed guide on my trip down the river was a small, fresh-complexioned man, who looked about sixty and surprised me by telling me that he was seventy-three. He was, I could see, very proud of the fact that he had reached that age and didn't look it. We got into conversation before the steamer sailed—'I knew you were a stranger, right away,' he said—and when I told him that I was keen to know something about the river, his eyes sparkled, and I knew that I had met the right man. In case you may think that my luck was phenomenal, I can assure you that very many men of his age are as knowledgeable as he was, for Glasgow men and Clydesiders generally, of the older generation, know their river.

The little man was a veritable encyclopaedia of Clyde knowledge. 'You'll want to know something about the shipyards,' he said; 'well, there's twenty-two of them on the Clyde. Mind you, you'll not see them all, for we're not going as far as Ardrossan; but you'll see most of them. I'll point them out as we reach them. By the way, I take it that you know something of the story of the Clyde?'

'All I know about the Clyde,' I told him, 'is that Clyde-built ships are known the world over.'

'I didn't mean that exactly. I mean the river's own story. It's a romance, sir, a romance. Think of it! About a hundred years ago only very small craft could come up the river, for it was very shallow, and full of sandbanks and other snags. This shallow river had long been a problem to Glasgow, for if Glasgow was to flourish, it had to have easy access to the sea. If that wasn't possible, then Glasgow had to have a port further down the river. The City Fathers decided that Dumbarton was the ideal place— that was away back in the seventeenth century —and would you believe it, sir, Dumbarton would have none of it!' The manner in which he said this indicated that he had a supreme contempt for the seventeenth-century inhabitants of Dumbarton, to miss such a chance. Then he went on:

'And why wouldn't Dumbarton consider this proposal? The people there said that prices would rise if sailors were coming about the town, and they didn't want that.' He snorted at the very thought of it.

'So the Town Council had a look at the other side of the river, and eventually bought a piece of ground from Sir Patrick Maxwell, of Newark Castle—you'll see the ruins of the castle as we get down the river—and a town and harbour was built. That town is Port-Glasgow to-day, the port of Glasgow, although it began as New Port; and the first dry dock for ships ever built in Scotland was made there. It was an unsatisfactory arrangement this having a port so far away from the city—it's about a dozen miles or more—and it was decided to deepen the bed of the river. You can realise that before the days of the steam dredger this must have been a long and difficult job. Before 1824, bucket dredgers were worked by hand, but after that steam dredgers were on the job, and have been on it ever since. That means that the largest ships in the world can now come up what was once a shallow stream, and that's what's meant by the saying "Glasgow made the Clyde, and the Clyde made Glasgow." '

We were now passing a huge crane. 'That can lift 130 tons,' he said proudly, as if he were personally responsible for this feat: 'and that's the Finnieston ferryboat just starting to move across the river.'

And so we sailed on, and all the while he kept pointing to various places of interest. 'That's the Queen's Dock and that's Prince's Dock. See these ships—they're Donaldson and Canadian Pacific liners. There's the Anchor Line berths down there, and yon's a Holt boat, the Blue Funnel boys. But—listen! Isn't that sweet music?'

The 'sweet music' to which he drew my attention was the sound of pneumatic riveting machines coming from a shipyard. 'That's Harland and Wolff's yard; you know, Belfast too.'

I didn't know but I let it pass.

'Yes that's grand music, and it's just as well that you didn't visit the Clyde some years ago, for you wouldn't have heard much of it then.

We had a bad time, sir, I can tell you, and it was heart-breaking to sail down here past more or less deserted and silent shipyards. Thank God that's past for a time, at least, and I hope for ever.' He seemed to feel this keenly, and did not speak for a minute or so.

Then he pointed again. 'See that there. That's Meadowside Granary—one of the finest in Britain. They can store over 30,000 tons of grain there. That shipyard on the other side is the famous Fairfield Company's yard. We're coming to Merklands Quay, where the foreign cattle are landed, and fruit too.'

'Forgive my interrupting you,' I said, 'but I've just been thinking that it must be a difficult job launching ships into this narrow channel.'

'It's not easy,' he said. 'You'll notice that they enter the river at an angle. Of course, it's a scientific job. The ships are held back by heavy drag chains that are coiled up, and it's a fine sight to see these chains uncoiling as the ship goes down the ways. Everything is calculated to a nicety.'

'And is there never an accident or a hitch?'

'It's rather strange that you should ask that at this point, for we're just approaching the yard of Alexander Stephen and Son—Stephens of Linthouse—where one of the worst disasters that ever happened on the Clyde took place. And it was at a launch. I saw it happen, for I was one of the spectators who lined the banks of the river to see the *Daphne* launched. That's about fifty-five years ago—the date was July 3, 1883, to be precise, and the day was a Tuesday. The *Daphne* was launched at half-past eleven in the forenoon, when the tide was high, and about 200 workmen were on board. She went down the ways all right, to the cheers of the crowds, and took the water perfectly—then, to our horror, she turned over on her side, and sank. Men dived overboard and swam for their lives, and small boats rushed to their assistance, but did not manage to pick them all up. Unfortunately, many of the workmen were below, and they were all drowned. In all 124 men lost their lives. It was a pitiful thing to see the ship lying in the river on her side when the tide went down, and for the next fortnight divers were busy looking for bodies. They got the ship refloated on July 19. It was a terrible affair, and I shall never forget that day. Fortunately, there's been nothing like it since, though there have been minor accidents at launches, such as the ship refusing to move, or sticking on the

ways. I've read somewhere that during the War
a cruiser or destroyer stuck in this way, and
wasn't launched until night, by the light of the
moon.'

In a chapter of this kind it is difficult to avoid
making what seems like a catalogue of docks
and shipyards, but as my guide pointed them
out, I feel I must mention them. We passed the
new Shieldhall Dock—it is about half a mile
long—and in succession the yards of Connell
and Company, the Blythswood Company,
Yarrow and Company, and Barclay, Curle and
Company. Passing Renfrew Ferry, we then
came to the yards of Simons and Company and
Lobnitz and Company, then Rothesay Dock,
and below it, the yard in which I was specially
interested—John Brown and Company, where
the sister ship to the *Queen Mary*, the *Queen
Elizabeth*, or, as she is not yet christened,
'Number 552' is gradually taking shape.

'Yes, there she is,' said my friend. 'There's a
lot to be done to her yet.' To me she looked like
a half-flensed whale, for she was not yet fully
plated—or did not appear to be from the
steamer—and I could still see some of her
ribs.

'I hope to see her launched,' my friend said.

'I saw the *Queen Mary* take the water, as well as the *Lusitania* and the *Aquitania*, for they also were built here. The greatest day of all, however, was when the *Queen Mary* sailed down the river for the first time. I was in a tug with a bunch of Pressmen and photographers. Our hearts were in our mouths when she began to swing across the river, and looked as if she were going to stick. But she didn't, and her progress down to the Firth was a triumph. If you could have seen the banks of the river that day you would have sworn that the entire population of the world was lining each side of the Clyde. Oh, that little place over there is Bowling—you can see some of the river steamers in the harbour—and there's the entrance to the Forth and Clyde Canal. It was on this canal that the first boat ever to be driven by steam was seen. She was the *Charlotte Dundas*, and began her career in 1802. It was not until 1812 that Henry Bell's *Comet* was built. Many people are under the impression that the *Comet* was the first steamboat, but actually the *Charlotte Dundas* had that honour. The *Comet* was the first steamboat to sail on the Clyde. By the way, there's a monument to Henry Bell over there (he pointed to a place which I learned is called

Dunglass), and that building there is Erskine House, now an hospital for limbless soldiers.'

The river had now become wider, and the channel was well marked by buoys. 'That's Dumbarton Rock' said my companion, and there was that tone in his voice that indicated that he had not quite forgiven the past inhabitants of Dumbarton for refusing to allow their town to become the port of Glasgow. 'The shipyard is Denny Brothers' place, and over there, among the hills, is Loch Lomond. That river running into the Clyde is the Leven, and it comes from Loch Lomond.

Some miles further on we passed Port Glasgow, and I saw the ruin of Newark Castle, as well as several more shipyards, among them Ferguson Brothers, who built the famous Antarctic ship *Discovery II*. On further to Greenock, where Scott's yard was pointed out, one of the most famous yards on the lower reaches of the Clyde, I was told, famed for naval and mercantile ships alike. 'That used to be a famous yard,' said my friend, pointing to another part. 'It was where Caird and Company built so many P.&O. ships. Then Harland and Wolff took it over, and later gave it up, and no more ships are built there now.'

So this is Glasgow!

I had reached the end of my journey, for I was to disembark at Greenock, where I was to catch a train back to Glasgow. My eye was held by a noble tower that shot into the sky, but otherwise the town looked drab. Yet, I have made it a rule never to judge a town by its waterfront, and in the case of Greenock, no one should. When I visited this town later, I found much to admire in it, and one of the things I shall always treasure is a view of the Firth I had from the top of a hill that is the highest point of what is known as the Lyle Road. There can be few finer views in Scotland.

Before I left the steamer and my most helpful friend who was going further—we are to meet again—I took a last look that day at the wide expanse of Firth, and the lovely hills piled up on the other side. I knew then that when Scotsmen speak of the glories of the Clyde, they are not boasting. They are merely stating a fact.

Chapter XVIII

Some time ago I read a symposium to which a number of well-known authors had contributed. The majority held that the most difficult thing in writing a book was beginning it. I am not a well-known author—in fact, I hardly dare to call myself an author on the strength of these few notes—but I disagree with that statement about the beginning of a book. To end a book is much more difficult.

I am finding it so. I have to end it here, yet having read over what I have written, I realise how much I have omitted. There are innumerable aspects of Glasgow life about which I know nothing. There are other aspects on which I have not touched, for, after all, I am a stranger, and a casual observer.

One thing, however, does give me a certain amount of satisfaction—I have justified my visit to Glasgow. When I set out on this 'voyage of discovery,' I felt in my heart that Glasgow could not possibly be as black as she is painted —and remember, the 'painters' are those who know little or nothing about the city. That feeling has been confirmed by what I have seen and heard. To those who still think of Glasgow as a dull, dismal, dirty city, peopled by 'savages,' I say—Come and see for yourselves, and realise how wrong you have been.

Glasgow has many problems to solve, industrial and social, just as all great cities have, and I have touched on none of these. It would have been an impertinence on my part to do so. This has been a deliberately light-hearted record of experiences that do not go beneath the surface: that is, except in one thing—the sterling worth of the Glasgow citizen. One has not to probe to find that.

This is not flattery, but fact. I was a stranger, and knew not a single soul in Glasgow, yet I have been here only a few months and I have made many friends. I have found nothing but kindness and consideration wherever I have gone. All sorts and conditions of people have shown me kindnesses, and the courtesy of railway officials, tram conductors, bus conductors, shop assistants, commissionaires and casual strangers met in the street or elsewhere, has been such that I shall never forget it.

In no city of the world have I experienced

such genuine hospitality. That may seem a large claim to make, nevertheless it is true. And this hospitality belongs to no particular class—it is general.

Then Glasgow is a city of which its inhabitants have every reason to feel proud. It has many fine streets, and many beautiful buildings. It is well-managed by those whose business it is to run it, and if it still has slums and foul spots— which seem inevitable in all cities—eyes are not being closed to such things.

It is a clean city, that is, as clean as any industrial city can be, and as I write I see every evidence of a determination to make it cleaner.

The stories concerning its wildness in the matter of gang-warfare and rowdyism are, like a certain report of the death of Mark Twain many years ago, 'very much exaggerated.' I have explored every part of Glasgow, both by day and by night, and I have seen no trace of this alleged gang-warfare. That fights have taken place, I do not doubt: that some misguided youths have slashed other equally misguided youths with razors I do not doubt either; there is evidence to prove those things. But I cannot help feeling that such occurrences have been magnified and grossly exaggerated.

I have visited some of the dance-halls whence such battles are said to emanate, and they seemed perfectly decorous to me. The one thing I did notice about them was that the dancing was vastly superior to the dancing I had seen at higher-class establishments.

Has Glasgow no faults? I hear you asking. Many, no doubt, but I did not come to Glasgow to find faults; I came to see the brighter side of the city's life, and I have seen it. I leave the faults to other pens.

I realise how inadequate this book is, but, at the same time, if I have missed many of the things that you may think should have been included as typical of Glasgow life, what I have included is the real Glasgow. Of that I am certain.

So I lay down my pen, with the hope that what I have written may have interested and, at times, amused you: and that it may help a little in dispelling some of the mistaken ideas that exist about a great and pleasant city.

PRINTED IN GREAT BRITAIN BY ROBERT MACLEHOSE AND CO., LTD.
THE UNIVERSITY PRESS, GLASGOW, FOR JACKSON, SON AND CO.
(BOOKSELLERS) LTD., PUBLISHERS TO THE UNIVERSITY, GLASGOW